The Baseball Book for Boys

Everything Young Readers Need to Know About the History, Rules, Tips, Trivia, Best Teams and Biographies of the Greatest Players of America's National Pastime

Bradley Simon

Table of Contents

Chapter One: A Brief History of Baseball: From Its Origins to the Modern Era 1

Chapter Two: The Basic Rules of Baseball: Understanding the Game 9

Chapter Three: Positions on the Field: Roles and Responsibilities 15

Chapter Four: Famous Ballparks: Exploring the Iconic Homes of Baseball 24

Chapter Five: Baseball's Greatest Players: Stories of the All-Time Greats .34

Chapter Six: Greatest Teams in Baseball History: Dynasties and Legends..56

Chapter Seven: The Most Amazing Games in Baseball History 63

Chapter Eight: The Art of Hitting: Techniques and Tips to Improve Your Swing 76

Chapter Nine: Pitching 101: The Basics of Throwing and Types of Pitches 82

Chapter Ten: Fielding Fundamentals: Mastering the Skills of Defense 88

Chapter Eleven: Base Running and Stealing: How Speed Can Win Games 94

Chapter Twelve: Baseball Movies and Books: Entertainment for Fans 100

Chapter Thirteen: Baseball Trivia 115

Chapter Fourteen: Rounding the Bases: Bringing It All Together 119

Chapter One:

A Brief History of Baseball: From Its Origins to the Modern Era

Step up to the plate and get ready to explore the great world of baseball! This amazing sport has captivated the hearts and minds of people for over a century. As we embark on this journey together, we'll dive deep into the history of baseball, tracing its roots from humble beginnings to the action-packed games we know and love today. So grab your glove, your cap, and your sense of adventure, and let's discover the incredible story behind one of the most popular sports in the world!

Baseball is a sport with deep roots in American history, dating back to the early 1800s. While there are many theories about its origins, most historians agree that baseball evolved from various bat-and-ball games played in England. The game we know today, however, has come a long way since its early beginnings. In this chapter, we'll dive into the fascinating history of baseball, exploring its origins, the evolution of the rules, the birth of professional leagues, and the unforgettable moments that have made it America's favorite pastime, all while keeping in mind our young audience of baseball enthusiasts aged 9 to 12.

The origins of baseball can be traced back to various bat-and-ball games played in England, such as cricket, rounders, and stoolball. These games were brought to North America by early settlers, and versions of these games were played by both children and adults throughout the American colonies. Many of these early games shared similarities with modern baseball, such as hitting a ball with a bat and running to bases to score points.

In the mid-19th century, baseball started to gain popularity in the United States. There was a growing interest in leisure activities, and people from all walks of life began to play baseball in their free time. The game was played on sandlots, open fields, and even city streets. One of the earliest recorded games took place in 1842, when a group of young men in Manhattan formed the New York Knickerbockers, a baseball club that played according to a set of rules developed by Alexander Cartwright.

Cartwright, a bank clerk and volunteer firefighter, is often referred to as the "father of modern baseball" due to his role in establishing many of the game's early rules. He and his fellow club members created a set of 20 rules for their version of the game, which they called "base ball." Some of these rules included having nine players on each team, the use of a diamond-shaped field with bases 90 feet apart, and the concept of "three strikes and you're out." Cartwright's rules were widely adopted by other clubs and are considered the foundation of modern baseball.

The first recorded baseball game played under these rules took place in 1846 in Hoboken, New Jersey, between the New York Knickerbockers and the New York Nine. The game was played on the Elysian Fields, a large park that was a popular spot for sporting events at the time. The New York Nine won the game with a score of 23 to 1, but this historic match marked the beginning of baseball's rise as a popular sport in the United States.

As baseball's popularity grew, so did the number of clubs and teams. Many of these clubs were made up of young professionals and businessmen who played the game in their spare time. These amateur teams often competed against one another in friendly matches and tournaments. By the late 1850s, baseball had become a popular spectator sport, with thousands of fans attending games and following their favorite teams.

The outbreak of the Civil War in 1861 had a significant impact on the spread of baseball throughout the United States. Soldiers from both the Union and Confederate armies played the game during their downtime, introducing it to new regions of the country. After the war, baseball's popularity continued to grow, and more organized leagues and associations began to form.

In 1869, the Cincinnati Red Stockings became the first openly professional baseball team. Owned by the brother of a prominent Cincinnati businessman, the Red Stockings recruited the best players from around the country and paid them salaries to play for the team. This marked a major shift in the sport, as more teams began to follow the Red Stockings' example and pay their players, leading to the establishment of professional baseball leagues.

The National Association of Professional Base Ball Players was formed in 1871, becoming the first professional baseball league in the United States. The league featured nine teams from cities across the country, including the Boston Red Stockings, the Chicago White Stockings, and the New York Mutuals. Over the next five years, the National Association struggled with issues such as gambling, player misconduct, and financial instability.

In response to these challenges, the National League of Professional Base Ball Clubs was established in 1876. The new league had stricter rules, a more structured schedule, and a stronger commitment to the integrity of the game. The National League's founding teams included the Boston Red Caps, the Chicago White Stockings, the Cincinnati Red Stockings, the Hartford Dark Blues, the Louisville Grays, the New York Mutuals, the Philadelphia Athletics, and the St. Louis Brown Stockings.

During the late 19th century and early 20th century, baseball continued to grow in popularity, and the sport saw many innovations and improvements. In 1884, the first World Series was played between the champions of the National League and the

American Association, a rival professional league that had been established in 1882. This tradition of a championship series between the two best teams in professional baseball would continue and evolve over time, becoming the modern-day World Series.

As baseball entered the 20th century, the game saw many changes that helped shape it into the sport we know today. In 1903, the American League was established as a rival to the National League, and the two leagues would compete against each other for dominance in the world of professional baseball. The first official World Series between the National League and the American League champions took place that same year, with the Boston Red Sox defeating the Pittsburgh Pirates in a thrilling eight-game series.

Throughout the early 1900s, baseball witnessed the rise of some of the game's most legendary players, including Ty Cobb, Babe Ruth, Lou Gehrig, and Honus Wagner. These players captivated fans with their incredible skills and larger-than-life personalities, helping to cement baseball's status as America's favorite pastime.

In 1947, Jackie Robinson made history when he became the first African-American player to play in the major leagues, breaking the sport's long-standing color barrier. Robinson's courage and determination paved the way for other talented African-American players to follow in his footsteps, and his impact on the game of baseball can still be felt today.

The second half of the 20th century saw baseball continue to grow and evolve, with new teams, stadiums, and unforgettable moments capturing the imaginations of fans around the world. In the 1960s and 70s, the sport underwent a period of expansion, with new teams being added to both the National and American leagues. The era also saw the introduction of the designated hitter rule in the American League, which allowed teams to use a player solely to bat in place of the pitcher.

Over the years, baseball has been home to countless memorable moments, from perfect games and no-hitters to record-breaking home runs and dramatic come-from-behind victories. Some of these unforgettable games have become the stuff of legend, such as the "Shot Heard 'Round the World" in 1951, when Bobby Thomson hit a walk-off home run to send the New York Giants to the World Series, or the 1988 World Series, when an injured Kirk Gibson hit a pinch-hit, game-winning home run for the Los Angeles Dodgers.

Today, baseball remains a beloved sport, enjoyed by millions of fans around the world. From its humble beginnings as a simple bat-and-ball game to the thrilling spectacle of modern professional baseball, the history of this great sport is filled with passion, excitement, and unforgettable moments. As new generations of players continue to take the field, the game of baseball continues to evolve and capture the hearts of fans everywhere.

In recent years, baseball has also seen an increase in international talent, with players from countries like the Dominican Republic, Japan, Venezuela, and Cuba making their mark on the sport. This influx of talent from around the world has added a new level of excitement and competition to the game, as players from diverse backgrounds bring their unique skills and styles of play to the field.

The rise of advanced statistics and data analysis, known as sabermetrics, has also had a significant impact on the game of baseball. Teams now use sophisticated computer models and data-driven strategies to evaluate player performance and make decisions about lineups, player acquisitions, and game strategy. This new approach to the game has led to innovative strategies and a deeper understanding of the factors that contribute to a team's success on the field.

Baseball has also made strides in the area of player safety, with new rules and equipment designed to protect players from injury. For example, recent rule changes have addressed the issue of home plate collisions, requiring runners to slide into home plate rather than crash into the catcher in an attempt to dislodge the ball. Additionally, improved helmet technology has helped reduce the risk of serious head injuries from being hit by a pitched ball.

As we look to the future, the game of baseball will undoubtedly continue to evolve and adapt to the changing world around it. New technologies, like virtual reality and advanced analytics, will further enhance the way the game is played, coached, and enjoyed by fans. And as young players continue to discover the joy and excitement of stepping up to the plate and swinging for the fences, the timeless appeal of baseball will endure for generations to come.

In this chapter, we've explored the rich history of baseball, from its origins as a simple bat-and-ball game played in the early 1800s to the thrilling spectacle of modern professional baseball. We've learned about the key figures who helped shape the sport, like Alexander Cartwright, the "father of modern baseball," and the legendary players who have left their mark on the game. We've also looked at the unforgettable moments and games that have captured the hearts of baseball fans throughout the years. With its deep roots in American history and its enduring appeal to fans of all ages, baseball truly is America's favorite pastime – a sport that connects us to our past while continuing to inspire us as we look toward the future.

Chapter Two:

The Basic Rules of Baseball: Understanding the Game

In this chapter, we'll cover the fundamental rules of baseball, helping you understand the game's structure and objectives. From the layout of the field to the roles of the players, we'll give you the essential knowledge to appreciate and enjoy America's favorite pastime.

The Baseball Field

A baseball field, also known as a diamond, consists of four bases: first base, second base, third base, and home plate. The bases are 90 feet apart from each other, forming a square. In the center of the diamond is the pitcher's mound, where the pitcher stands to throw the ball to the batter at home plate. The field is divided into two main areas: the infield, which includes the diamond and the area within it, and the outfield, which extends from the infield to the outer fence.

The Objective of the Game

The main objective of baseball is to score more runs than the opposing team. A run is scored when a player on the batting team successfully moves around all four bases and crosses home plate. The team with the most runs at the end of the game wins.

Innings, Outs, and Strikes

A baseball game is divided into nine innings, with each inning consisting of two halves: the top and the bottom. In each half-inning, one team is on offense (batting), while the other team is on defense (fielding). Each team gets a turn at bat in every inning.

When a team is batting, their goal is to get players on base and advance them around the bases to score runs. The fielding team's objective is to get three outs, which ends the half-inning and allows them to switch to offense.

An out can occur in several ways:

A strikeout:

A batter gets three strikes (swinging at and missing the ball, or not swinging at a pitch that is in the strike zone).

A flyout:

A batter hits the ball into the air, and a fielder catches it before it touches the ground.

A groundout:

A batter hits the ball on the ground, and a fielder throws the ball to a base before the runner arrives.

A force out:

A fielder touches a base with the ball before the runner reaches it, forcing the runner out.

A tag out:

A fielder tags a runner with the ball while the runner is not touching a base.

The Batting Order and Substitutions

Each team has a lineup of nine players who take turns batting in a specific order. This batting order remains constant throughout the game, and players must bat in their designated spot. However, substitutions are allowed, with the new player taking the replaced player's spot in the batting order.

Baserunning and Stealing

Once a batter reaches base safely, they become a baserunner. The goal of the baserunner is to advance around the bases and eventually cross home plate to score a run. Baserunners can advance on a hit, a walk (when the pitcher throws four balls outside the strike zone), or a steal (when the runner advances to the next base while the pitcher is throwing the ball to the batter).

The Pitcher-Batter Duel

One of the most exciting aspects of baseball is the duel between the pitcher and the batter. The pitcher's goal is to throw the ball past the batter, either by striking them out or inducing a weak hit that results in an out. The batter's objective is to hit the ball into the field of play, allowing them to reach base and potentially advance other baserunners.

Now that you have a solid understanding of the basic rules of baseball, you're ready to dive deeper into the game. In the next chapter, we'll explore the different positions on the field, each with its own unique responsibilities and skills. Understanding these positions will help you appreciate the strategy and teamwork involved in baseball.

Pitch Counts and Balls

In addition to strikes, a pitcher can also throw balls. A ball occurs when the pitch is outside the strike zone and the batter doesn't swing at it. If a pitcher throws four balls to a batter, the batter is awarded a "walk" and gets to advance to first base.

The Strike Zone

The strike zone is an imaginary box over home plate, extending from the midpoint between the batter's shoulders and the top of their pants down to their knees. The width of the strike zone is the width of home plate, which is 17 inches. If a pitch passes through the strike zone and the batter doesn't swing, it's called a strike. If a batter swings and misses, it's also a strike, regardless of whether the pitch was in the strike zone.

Fouls and Fair Balls

When a batter hits the ball, it can either be a fair ball or a foul ball. A fair ball is any ball that lands in the field of play, between the two foul lines that run from home plate through first and third bases to the outfield fence. If a ball lands outside these lines or is touched in foul territory, it's considered a foul ball. Foul balls count as strikes, but a batter can't strike out on a foul ball unless they bunt (intentionally tap the ball without swinging hard).

The Role of the Umpires

In a baseball game, there are usually four umpires who are responsible for enforcing the rules and making decisions on the field. The home plate umpire stands behind the catcher and calls balls and strikes. The other three umpires are positioned in the infield and outfield to make decisions on plays at the bases, fair and foul balls, and other game situations.

Extra Innings and Tiebreakers

If the game is tied after nine innings, extra innings are played to determine the winner. Each extra inning is played just like a regular inning, with both teams getting a chance to bat. The game continues until one team has more runs than the other at the end of a completed inning.

The Designated Hitter (DH) Rule

In the American League, teams are allowed to use a designated hitter (DH) in place of the pitcher in the batting order.

The DH is a player who bats but does not play a position in the field. This rule was implemented in 1973 to increase offense in the game, as pitchers are generally not strong hitters. The National League does not use the DH rule, so pitchers must bat in the lineup.

Now that you have a deeper understanding of the basic rules and structure of baseball, you'll be able to follow the action and enjoy the game even more. In the next chapter, we'll delve into the specific roles and responsibilities of each position on the field, giving you a comprehensive understanding of how the game is played and the strategies employed by teams.

Chapter Three:

Positions on the Field:

Roles and Responsibilities

In this chapter, we'll explore the different positions on the baseball field, helping you understand the unique responsibilities and skills of each player. Knowing these positions will give you a better appreciation of the teamwork and strategy involved in baseball.

Pitcher (P)

A pitcher is one of the most important players on a baseball team. They stand on a slightly elevated mound in the middle of the field and throw the ball to the catcher behind home plate. The pitcher's main goal is to get the batter out by either striking them out, forcing them to hit a ball that can be caught by a fielder, or making them hit a ground ball that can be thrown to a base for an out.

Pitchers have a lot of responsibilities on the field. They need to have great control over their pitches, and they often have a variety of different pitches they can throw, like fastballs, curveballs, and changeups. A good pitcher is able to mix up their pitches to keep batters guessing and off-balance. They also need to be aware of any base runners, as they can try to steal a base while the pitcher is focused on the batter. Being a pitcher takes skill, concentration, and a strong arm, making it a challenging but exciting position to play in baseball.

Catcher (C)

A catcher is another crucial player on a baseball team, working closely with the pitcher to form what's known as the "battery." Positioned behind home plate, the catcher wears special protective gear, including a helmet, mask, chest protector, and shin guards, to keep them safe from any stray balls or collisions. Catchers play a vital role in both defense and offense, so they must be skilled, quick-thinking, and have a strong arm.

On defense, catchers are responsible for receiving the pitcher's throws, called "pitches." They help the pitcher choose which type of pitch to throw and give signals to indicate their choice. Catchers also play an essential role in preventing base runners from stealing bases by quickly throwing the ball to the appropriate base. On offense, catchers must also be good batters, as they take their turn at the plate to hit the ball and score runs for their team. Overall, being a catcher requires a combination of strength, agility, and strategic thinking, making it a challenging and rewarding position in the game of baseball.

First Baseman (1B)

A first baseman is an essential player on the defensive side of a baseball team, and they are stationed at the first base, which is one of the four corners of the baseball diamond. Their main responsibility is to catch balls thrown to them by other players on the field, as well as to tag out the base runners who are trying to reach first base safely. They need to have quick reflexes and good hand-eye coordination, as well as the ability to stretch and make difficult catches.

Aside from their defensive duties, the first baseman also plays a role in the offense. When it's their turn to bat, they aim to hit the ball and reach base safely, helping their team score runs. Often, first basemen are tall and have a strong build, as this helps them make catches and stretch out to receive throws from their teammates. Good first basemen can make a huge difference in a game, as they play a critical part in getting outs and preventing the opposing team from scoring.

Second Baseman (2B)

The second baseman is another important player on a baseball team, positioned between first and second base, closer to the second base. This player has a crucial role in the infield and is involved in various plays throughout the game. Their responsibilities include fielding ground balls hit in their direction, catching line drives, and participating in double plays. The second baseman needs to have quick footwork and excellent hand-eye coordination to make fast and accurate throws to first base or to other bases for outs.

In addition to their defensive duties, second basemen also contribute to the offense when it's their turn to bat. They aim to hit the ball and reach base safely, helping their team score runs. Second basemen are typically smaller and faster than first basemen, as they need to cover more ground and quickly react to the ball. A skilled second baseman can be a game-changer, as their agility and quick decision-making can stop the opposing team from scoring and help turn the tide of the game.

Third Baseman (3B)

The third baseman is a key player in the infield, positioned near the third base, and is sometimes called the "hot corner." This nickname comes from the fact that batters often hit hard grounders and line drives down the third-base line, so the third baseman has to be ready for some sizzling action! To play this position, a person needs to have quick reflexes, a strong arm, and a fearless attitude, as they might have to catch balls that are hit at lightning-fast speeds.

Defensively, the third baseman's job is to field any balls hit towards their side of the field and make strong, accurate throws to first base or other bases to get outs. They also need to be prepared to catch pop-ups and work with the shortstop on double plays. On offense, third basemen are typically strong hitters who can hit for power and drive in runs. They need to be well-rounded athletes, as their position requires both quick thinking and strength. A great third baseman can make a huge difference in a game by preventing runs from being scored and contributing to their team's offensive attack.

Shortstop (SS)

The shortstop is an essential player on the baseball field, positioned between the second and third bases. This position is often considered the captain of the infield due to the amount of ground they need to cover and the crucial plays they are involved in. A shortstop must have quick reflexes, a strong arm, and great agility to excel in this role. Being able to make split-second decisions is a valuable skill for a shortstop, as they are often responsible for deciding where to throw the ball in high-pressure situations.

Shortstops are involved in numerous defensive plays, such as fielding ground balls, catching line drives, and turning double plays. They need to communicate effectively with the second baseman, third baseman, and the outfielders to ensure the best possible outcome for their team. A shortstop is also expected to have a good range, meaning they can quickly move to either side to reach balls that other infielders might not be able to get to. On offense, shortstops are typically skilled at both hitting for contact and stealing bases. Their speed and athleticism make them valuable assets on the basepaths and help them score runs for their team.

Left Fielder (LF)

The left fielder is an outfielder who plays on the left side of the baseball field, near the foul line. This position is crucial in the outfield because many right-handed batters tend to hit the ball towards the left side of the field. As a result, a left fielder must be prepared to catch fly balls, chase down ground balls, and make accurate throws back to the infield. A strong arm and quick reflexes are essential skills for a left fielder, as they often have to make long throws to prevent runners from advancing on the basepaths.

Left fielders are also responsible for backing up the third baseman and shortstop on balls hit to their side of the field. This teamwork helps prevent extra bases from being taken by the opposing team. On offense, left fielders are usually expected to be strong hitters. They often possess power and can hit the ball for extra bases or even home runs. Speed is also an essential attribute for left fielders, as it enables them to cover more ground in the outfield and be a threat on the basepaths when they're up to bat..

Center Fielder (CF)

The center fielder is an outfielder who plays right in the middle of the outfield, between the left fielder and the right fielder. This position is often considered the captain of the outfield due to its central location and the unique perspective it provides on the entire field. Center fielders need to be great athletes, as they are responsible for covering a large area and making plays on balls hit to all parts of the field. They must have excellent speed, agility, and quick reactions to track down fly balls and grounders that make it into the outfield.

On top of their defensive duties, center fielders are also responsible for communicating with their fellow outfielders to prevent collisions and ensure that everyone knows who is going after a ball. This coordination is essential for keeping the outfield running smoothly and avoiding mistakes that could lead to extra bases for the opposing team. On offense, center fielders are typically strong hitters who can make contact and get on base. They are often good base runners, using their speed to steal bases and score runs, which helps their team rack up points and win games.

Right Fielder (RF)

Right field is an important position on the baseball field, located in the outfield near the right foul line. The player who occupies this position is called the right fielder. They have some key responsibilities to help their team win, and they need to be quick on their feet, have good throwing skills, and be able to catch fly balls with ease. Just like the other outfielders, the right fielder needs to cover a lot of ground to keep the opposing team from getting extra bases.

The main responsibility of a right fielder is to catch any fly balls or line drives that come their way. They also need to be alert and ready to quickly field ground balls that roll into the outfield. Right fielders should have a strong arm, as they often have to make long throws to the infield to prevent runners from advancing. Communication is also crucial, as they need to work together with the other outfielders and infielders to make sure everyone knows who is going after the ball. All in all, the right fielder plays an important role in the team's defense, helping to keep the other team from scoring and making some awesome catches along the way!

Now that you're familiar with the positions on the field, let's take a closer look at some of the additional responsibilities and skills that players often develop to excel in their roles.

Position Flexibility

While each player has a primary position, it's not uncommon for them to learn multiple positions to help their team. This flexibility can be valuable when a teammate gets injured or when the team needs to adjust its strategy. For example, some outfielders can play all three outfield positions, while some infielders can play both second base and shortstop.

Backup Catcher

In addition to the starting catcher, most teams have a backup catcher on their roster. The backup catcher is crucial in case the starting catcher gets injured or needs a break. They must be ready to step in at any time and have a good understanding of the team's pitching staff and defensive strategies.

Utility Players

A utility player is someone who can play multiple positions on the field. These players are valuable assets to their team, as they can fill in at various positions when needed. Utility players are often versatile athletes who have honed their skills in several areas of the game.

Platooning

Sometimes, teams will use a strategy called platooning, where two players share playing time at a specific position based on the opposing pitcher. For example, a team may have a right-handed batter and a left-handed batter share playing time at first base. The right-handed batter would start against left-handed pitchers, while the left-handed batter would start against right-handed pitchers. This strategy takes advantage of the fact that it's generally more challenging for batters to hit against pitchers who throw with the same hand they bat with.

Pitcher Specializations

While we've covered the basic role of a pitcher, it's important to know that there are different types of pitchers on a team. Starting pitchers usually pitch every fifth game and are expected to throw multiple innings, while relief pitchers come in for shorter stints later in the game. Relief pitchers often have specific roles, such as setup men, who pitch in the late innings before the team's closer, and closers, who specialize in getting the final outs of a close game to secure a win.

Now that you have a deeper understanding of the various roles and responsibilities of baseball players, you can better appreciate the teamwork and strategy involved in the game. In the next chapter, we'll dive into the greatest teams and players in baseball history, helping you learn about the legends who have shaped America's favorite pastime.

Chapter Four:

Famous Ballparks: Exploring the Iconic Homes of Baseball

Baseball isn't just about the players on the field; it's also about the places where they play. In this chapter, we'll take a tour of some of the most iconic ballparks in baseball history. These stadiums are filled with stories, memories, and unique features that make each one special.

Fenway Park - Boston Red Sox

Fenway Park, located in Boston, Massachusetts, is the oldest active Major League Baseball stadium and home to the Boston Red Sox since 1912. This iconic ballpark is packed with cool features that make it unique and exciting for both players and fans.

The most famous part of Fenway Park is the Green Monster, a massive 37-foot-tall wall in left field. This towering wall challenges hitters to hit a home run over it and fielders to make incredible catches. In right field, there's Pesky's Pole, named after former Red Sox player Johnny Pesky. It's the shortest distance to hit a home run in the major leagues, making it a favorite target for left-handed hitters.

Another interesting feature of Fenway Park is The Triangle, a uniquely shaped area in center field that can create exciting and challenging plays. And don't forget the Lone Red Seat, which marks the spot of the longest home run ever hit inside Fenway Park by the legendary Ted Williams.

Fenway Park is a living piece of baseball history, filled with amazing stories and memories. If you ever have the chance to visit, make sure to take in the atmosphere and appreciate this one-of-a-kind ballpark.

Wrigley Field - Chicago Cubs

Wrigley Field, located in Chicago, Illinois, is another iconic and historic ballpark in Major League Baseball. Home to the Chicago Cubs since 1914, Wrigley Field is the second oldest active MLB stadium, right behind Fenway Park. This classic ballpark has some awesome features that make it special for both players and fans.

One of the most famous parts of Wrigley Field is its ivy-covered outfield walls. The thick, green ivy gives the ballpark a unique, old-timey feel and can make fielding extra challenging when the ball gets lost in the leaves. Another cool feature is the manual scoreboard in center field. This giant, green scoreboard is one of the last remaining manually operated scoreboards in the major leagues, with workers inside updating the scores using metal plates.

Wrigley Field is also known for its iconic red marquee sign at the main entrance, displaying the words "Wrigley Field, Home of Chicago Cubs" in white letters. This sign has become a symbol of the ballpark and a favorite spot for fans to take pictures.

Visiting Wrigley Field is like stepping back in time and experiencing the rich history of baseball. If you ever get the chance to go, make sure to take a moment to enjoy the unique atmosphere and appreciate this legendary ballpark.

Yankee Stadium - New York Yankees

Yankee Stadium, located in the Bronx, New York City, is the famous home of the New York Yankees, one of the most successful and storied teams in Major League Baseball. The current Yankee Stadium, which opened in 2009, was built right across the street from the original stadium, often referred to as "The House that Ruth Built," in honor of the legendary Babe Ruth.

One of the most iconic features of Yankee Stadium is Monument Park, an outdoor museum located behind the center field wall. This special area honors some of the greatest players in Yankees history, with plaques and retired numbers on display for fans to explore. Another cool feature is the massive, high-definition video board in center field, which is one of the largest in the major leagues, giving fans an incredible view of replays, stats, and other exciting content.

Yankee Stadium is also known for its signature façade, a series of white, arched panels that run along the top of the stadium. This distinctive design element pays homage to the original stadium and adds a touch of classic elegance to the modern ballpark.

If you ever have the opportunity to visit Yankee Stadium, take a moment to appreciate the rich history and the exciting atmosphere that surrounds you. From the cheers of passionate fans to the powerful legacy of the team, this ballpark truly captures the spirit of America's National Pastime.

Dodger Stadium - Los Angeles Dodgers

Dodger Stadium, nestled in the hills of Los Angeles, California, is the legendary home of the Los Angeles Dodgers. Since opening in 1962, this iconic ballpark has been the center of excitement for baseball fans on the West Coast. Dodger Stadium is currently the third oldest active MLB stadium and has some cool features that make it a favorite among players and fans alike.

One of the most famous aspects of Dodger Stadium is its breathtaking view of the San Gabriel Mountains beyond the outfield. On a clear day, you can see the mountains towering in the distance, creating a beautiful backdrop for the action on the field. The stadium also has a unique terraced layout, with multiple levels of seating that provide fans with great views from every angle.

Dodger Stadium is known for its delicious ballpark food,

especially the famous Dodger Dog. This tasty, foot-long hot dog has become a fan favorite and is a must-try when you visit the stadium. Don't forget to grab a bag of salty peanuts or some sweet cotton candy to complete your ballpark snack experience.

If you ever get the chance to visit Dodger Stadium, be sure to take in the stunning views, enjoy the delicious food, and soak up the exciting atmosphere of a Dodgers game. With its unique blend of natural beauty and thrilling baseball action, this legendary ballpark is a true gem of the major leagues.

PNC Park - Pittsburgh Pirates

PNC Park, situated in Pittsburgh, Pennsylvania, proudly hosts the Pittsburgh Pirates and offers an unforgettable experience for baseball fans. Opened in 2001, PNC Park is considered one of the most beautiful ballparks in Major League Baseball, and it's packed with exciting features that will have you cheering for more.

Get ready to be amazed by the stunning view of downtown Pittsburgh and the Roberto Clemente Bridge just beyond the outfield. This picturesque scene makes PNC Park a truly special place to watch a game. And when it comes to seating, there's not a bad spot in the house! The intimate design of the stadium makes you feel close to the action no matter where you sit.

At PNC Park, the fun doesn't stop at the game itself. The ballpark is filled with cool activities for fans of all ages. Check out the interactive playground and test your skills at the various games and challenges. And don't forget to grab a bite to eat! From mouthwatering burgers to tasty nachos, there's something for everyone to enjoy.

If you ever find yourself at a Pirates game in PNC Park, make sure to take the time to explore the ballpark and soak in the incredible views. With its unbeatable atmosphere, this modern stadium is sure to leave a lasting impression on any baseball fan.

Oracle Park - San Francisco Giants

Welcome to Oracle Park, the incredible home of the San Francisco Giants! Located in San Francisco, California, this fantastic ballpark opened its doors in 2000 and has been captivating baseball fans ever since. Oracle Park is truly one of a kind, and here's why:

First, you can't miss the extraordinary view of the San Francisco Bay! With the bay just beyond the right field wall, this picturesque scene is a perfect backdrop for baseball action. Keep an eye out for "splash hits," when a player hits a home run that lands in the water. It's always a thrill to see fans in kayaks and boats racing to grab the souvenir!

Next, you'll love exploring the unique features of the stadium. Take a stroll through the @Café, a social media hub where fans can share their love for the Giants and baseball. Or wander through the Giants Garden, a special area where fruits and vegetables are grown to use in the ballpark's delicious dishes.

Speaking of food, you won't want to miss the tasty treats that Oracle Park has to offer. From classic hot dogs and garlic fries to clam chowder in a sourdough bread bowl, there's something for everyone's taste buds.

So, if you ever find yourself at a Giants game in Oracle Park, be prepared for an unforgettable experience. With its jaw-dropping views and exciting atmosphere, this ballpark is truly a home run for baseball fans of all ages.

Camden Yards - Baltimore Orioles

Camden Yards, an amazing ballpark in Baltimore, Maryland, is where the Baltimore Orioles have been playing ball since 1992. This awesome stadium is known for its retro design and has some really cool features that make it stand out from the rest.

As you enter Camden Yards, you'll notice the B&O Warehouse, a huge brick building that sits just beyond right field. This historic structure adds a touch of old-school charm to the ballpark and serves as a unique backdrop for the game. There's even a flag court located in the outfield, where you can see the flags of all 30 Major League Baseball teams flying high.

When it comes to food, Camden Yards has got you covered! Be sure to try the famous crab cakes, a tasty local favorite that you won't want to miss. And if you're looking for something sweet, the snowballs (shaved ice with flavored syrup) are a perfect treat on a hot summer day.

Camden Yards is also known for its family-friendly

atmosphere, so there's plenty to do for fans of all ages. Check out the Kids' Corner, an interactive play area filled with fun games and activities, or visit the Orioles Hall of Fame to learn about the team's legendary players.

If you ever get the chance to see a game at Camden Yards, you're in for a real treat. With its unique blend of history and modern design, this ballpark is a must-visit destination for baseball fans everywhere.

Coors Field - Colorado Rockies

Get ready for an adventure at Coors Field, the spectacular home of the Colorado Rockies! Located in Denver, Colorado, this ballpark has been welcoming baseball fans since 1995, and it's got some awesome surprises in store for you.

Coors Field is nestled in the heart of downtown Denver, with the stunning Rocky Mountains in the distance. This jaw-dropping view is sure to take your breath away as you watch the game unfold. The stadium is also known for its high altitude, which can cause the baseball to travel farther, making it a haven for home run hitters and a thrilling experience for fans!

You won't want to miss the unique features that make Coors Field stand out. For example, the famous row of purple seats in the upper deck marks exactly one mile above sea level – now that's pretty cool! And if you're looking for some fun between innings, check out the interactive games and activities located throughout the ballpark.

When it's time to refuel, Coors Field has plenty of delicious options to choose from. Be sure to try the Rocky Mountain oysters, a local delicacy that's not for the faint of heart, or grab a slice of pizza and a cold drink to enjoy during the game.

So, if you ever have the chance to catch a Rockies game at Coors Field, prepare to be amazed by the stunning scenery and exciting atmosphere. This one-of-a-kind ballpark is truly a home run for baseball fans young and old alike.

Citi Field - New York Mets

Welcome to Citi Field, the awesome ballpark where the New York Mets call home! Located in Queens, New York, Citi Field has been entertaining baseball fans since 2009, and it's packed with fun and excitement for everyone.

One of the coolest things about Citi Field is its nod to the Mets' history. You'll find the Jackie Robinson Rotunda, a grand entrance dedicated to the legendary player who broke the color barrier in baseball. This area pays tribute to Robinson's impact on the game and his enduring legacy.

Citi Field has plenty of action both on and off the field. For young fans, make sure to check out the Fan Fest area, which features a mini baseball field, a batting cage, and a dunk tank. You can even meet Mr. Met, the team's beloved mascot, and snap a photo together!

Of course, you can't talk about Citi Field without mentioning the food. The stadium offers a wide variety of tasty options, like the fan-favorite Shake Shack burgers or the mouthwatering Fuku chicken sandwiches. Don't forget to grab some popcorn or a soft pretzel to snack on during the game!

So, if you find yourself at a Mets game in Citi Field, be prepared for an unforgettable day. From the amazing history to the thrilling baseball action, this modern ballpark has something for everyone to enjoy.

Progressive Field - Cleveland Guardians

Step right up to Progressive Field, the fantastic home of the Cleveland Guardians! Located in downtown Cleveland, Ohio, Progressive Field has been a favorite destination for baseball fans since 1994, and it's full of surprises that'll make your visit unforgettable.

One of the best things about Progressive Field is its downtown location. Surrounded by the bustling city, the stadium offers awesome views of the Cleveland skyline. And, with its modern design and comfortable seating, you'll have a great view of the game from any spot in the ballpark.

Progressive Field is also packed with cool attractions for kids. Be sure to visit the Kids Clubhouse, a two-story play area with interactive games and activities. You can even measure your own pitch speed or try your hand at batting in the mini-dugout!

When hunger strikes, you're in for a treat at Progressive Field. Chow down on some delicious local favorites like the spicy nachos or the scrumptious grilled cheese sandwiches. And don't forget to save room for dessert – the funnel cakes and ice cream are not to be missed!

So, if you ever have the chance to catch a Guardians game at Progressive Field, get ready for a day full of fun and excitement. With its impressive views and family-friendly atmosphere, this ballpark is a true winner for baseball fans of all ages.

Each of these ballparks holds a special place in the hearts of baseball fans, offering unique features and unforgettable experiences. Visiting these iconic stadiums is a dream come true for many young players, and experiencing the history and atmosphere can inspire a lifelong love of the game. In the next chapter, we'll learn about staying safe and healthy while playing baseball, so you can enjoy the sport to the fullest.

Chapter Five:

Baseball's Greatest Players: Stories of the All-Time Greats

The Baseball Hall of Fame in Cooperstown, New York, is a place where the greatest players in the history of the sport are honored and remembered. In this chapter, we'll learn about some of the legendary Hall of Famers whose amazing stories and incredible skills have left a lasting impact on the game.

Babe Ruth - The Sultan of Swat

Babe Ruth, also known as "The Great Bambino" or "The Sultan of Swat," was one of the most legendary baseball players of all time. Born as George Herman Ruth Jr. on February 6, 1895, in Baltimore, Maryland, he grew up to become a larger-than-life figure in the world of baseball. Ruth played for three Major League Baseball teams throughout his career, but he's most famous for his time with the New York Yankees.

Babe Ruth was a powerhouse on the field, known for his incredible home runs and amazing pitching skills. He started his career as a pitcher for the Boston Red Sox, where he helped lead the team to three World Series titles. But when he joined the New York Yankees, he switched to the outfield and became a home run hero. Ruth hit an astonishing 714 home runs during his career, a record that stood for almost 40 years until Hank Aaron broke it in 1974.

Off the field, Babe Ruth was known for his big personality and love for the game. He always had a smile on his face and enjoyed entertaining fans with his playful antics. Ruth's incredible talent, charisma, and dedication to baseball made him a true icon, and his legacy continues to inspire young players today. If you ever find yourself stepping up to the plate, just remember the spirit of Babe Ruth and swing for the fences!

Jackie Robinson - Breaking the Color Barrier

Jackie Robinson was a trailblazer in the world of baseball, a true hero who changed the game forever. Born on January 31, 1919, in Cairo, Georgia, Robinson grew up to become an extraordinary athlete and an important figure in the fight for equality. He made history in 1947 when he joined the Brooklyn Dodgers and became the first African American to play in Major League Baseball.

What made Jackie Robinson such a special player? Not only was he incredibly talented on the field, but he also faced tough challenges with courage and determination. At the time, baseball was segregated, and African American players were only allowed to play in the Negro Leagues. When Robinson joined the Dodgers, he broke the color barrier and opened the door for other talented players to follow in his footsteps.

Robinson faced racism and discrimination, but he never backed down. He proved that talent and hard work mattered more than the color of his skin. As a second baseman, Robinson was an amazing hitter, a fast runner, and a skilled fielder. During his career, he won Rookie of the Year, was named an All-Star six times, and helped lead the Dodgers to a World Series championship in 1955. Today, we remember Jackie Robinson as a true legend, both on and off the field. His courage, talent, and determination inspire us all to stand up against injustice and strive for a better future.

Lou Gehrig - The Iron Horse

Lou Gehrig, known as "The Iron Horse," was a remarkable baseball player who left an unforgettable mark on the sport. Born on June 19, 1903, in New York City, Gehrig grew up with a passion for baseball and went on to become one of the greatest players of all time. As a key member of the New York Yankees, Gehrig played alongside the legendary Babe Ruth, forming an unstoppable duo that brought the team great success.

Gehrig was famous for his incredible durability and consistency. He set a record by playing in 2,130 consecutive games, a streak that lasted for 14 years and wasn't broken until Cal Ripken Jr. surpassed it in 1995. This amazing accomplishment earned Gehrig the nickname "The Iron Horse." As a powerful hitter and an excellent first baseman, Gehrig was a force to be reckoned with on the field. He had a career batting average of .340, hit 493 home runs, and helped the Yankees win six World Series titles.

Tragically, Lou Gehrig's life and career were cut short by a rare and devastating disease called amyotrophic lateral sclerosis (ALS), which is now often referred to as Lou Gehrig's disease. In 1939, at the age of 36, Gehrig was forced to retire from baseball due to his illness. On July 4th of that year, he gave an emotional farewell speech at Yankee Stadium, where he famously declared himself "the luckiest man on the face of the Earth."

Lou Gehrig's courage and perseverance in the face of adversity have made him an enduring hero in the world of baseball. His incredible achievements on the field and his unwavering spirit continue to inspire young players to strive for greatness, no matter the obstacles they may face.

Hank Aaron - Hammerin' Hank

Hank Aaron, often called "Hammerin' Hank," was a baseball superstar who left an indelible mark on the sport. Born on February 5, 1934, in Mobile, Alabama, Aaron overcame humble beginnings and racial barriers to become one of the most accomplished players in Major League Baseball history. Playing mainly for the

Milwaukee/Atlanta Braves and finishing his career with the Milwaukee Brewers, Hank Aaron set records and inspired countless fans with his incredible skills on the field.

As an outstanding hitter, Aaron's main claim to fame was his extraordinary ability to hit home runs. In his amazing career, he hit 755 home runs, surpassing Babe Ruth's long-standing record of 714. Aaron held the home run record for 33 years until it was broken by Barry Bonds in 2007. In addition to his home run prowess, Aaron also excelled in other aspects of the game, including hitting for average, fielding, and base running.

Off the field, Hank Aaron faced many challenges, including racism and discrimination. As he neared Babe Ruth's home run record, Aaron received hate mail and threats from those who didn't want to see an African American player break the record. Despite these obstacles, Aaron remained focused on his goals and continued to demonstrate grace and determination throughout his career.

Today, Hank Aaron is remembered as a true legend in the world of baseball. His unwavering commitment to excellence, both on and off the field, serves as an inspiration to young players everywhere. By breaking barriers and shattering records, Aaron showed that with hard work, dedication, and perseverance, anything is possible.

Sandy Koufax - The Left Arm of God

Sandy Koufax, also known as "The Left Arm of God," was a

dazzling pitcher who amazed baseball fans with his talent and skill on the mound. Born on December 30, 1935, in Brooklyn, New York, Koufax discovered his love for baseball at a young age and went on to become one of the most dominant pitchers in Major League Baseball history. Playing his entire career for the Brooklyn/Los Angeles Dodgers, Koufax quickly earned a reputation as a force to be reckoned with on the field.

Koufax's pitching prowess was truly awe-inspiring. With a blazing fastball and a wicked curveball, he left opposing batters scratching their heads in disbelief. During his 12-year career, Koufax won three Cy Young Awards, which are given to the best pitcher in each league. He also pitched four no-hitters, including a perfect game, which is when a pitcher doesn't allow any opposing batters to reach base during the entire game.

One of the most impressive aspects of Sandy Koufax's career was his performance in the World Series. Koufax helped lead the Dodgers to four World Series titles and was named the World Series Most Valuable Player twice. His incredible ability to step up under pressure made him a true legend on the baseball diamond.

Sandy Koufax's legacy continues to inspire young players today. His dedication to the game, his incredible talent, and his humble demeanor serve as a shining example of what it means to be a great athlete. As one of the most celebrated left-handed pitchers in baseball history, Koufax's name will forever be synonymous with greatness.

Willie Mays - The Say Hey Kid

Willie Mays, nicknamed "The Say Hey Kid," was a baseball phenomenon who left fans in awe with his amazing skills on the field. Born on May 6, 1931, in Westfield, Alabama, Mays grew up with a deep love for baseball and went on to become one of the most celebrated players in Major League Baseball history. Playing mostly for the New York/San Francisco Giants, and finishing his career with the New York Mets, Mays dazzled fans with his incredible talent and athleticism.

Willie Mays was an all-around superstar, excelling at every aspect of the game. As a batter, Mays was known for his powerful swing and ability to hit the ball to all fields. He finished his career with an impressive 660 home runs, which ranks him fifth on the all-time list. In addition to his prowess at the plate, Mays was an extraordinary fielder, often making jaw-dropping catches in center field that left spectators in disbelief.

One of Mays' most iconic moments occurred during the 1954 World Series when he made "The Catch," an over-the-shoulder grab while sprinting towards the center field wall. This incredible play is still considered one of the best defensive plays in baseball history. Mays' ability to perform in the clutch helped the Giants win the World Series that year, and he went on to become a 24-time All-Star and two-time National League MVP.

Willie Mays' impact on the game of baseball is immeasurable. His incredible skills, boundless enthusiasm, and love for the sport serve as an inspiration for young players everywhere. As one of the greatest all-around players in baseball history, Mays will forever be remembered for his extraordinary contributions to America's favorite pastime.

Ted Williams - The Splendid Splinter

Ted Williams, often referred to as "The Splendid Splinter" or "The Kid," was a remarkable baseball player who wowed fans with his incredible skill as a hitter. Born on August 30, 1918, in San Diego, California, Williams found his calling in baseball and went on to become one of the best hitters in Major League Baseball history. Playing his entire career for the Boston Red Sox, Williams built a legacy that would inspire generations of baseball fans and players alike.

What set Ted Williams apart from other players was his extraordinary ability to hit the baseball with precision and power. As a left-handed batter, Williams had a keen eye for the strike zone and was known for his patience at the plate. He finished his career with a remarkable .344 batting average and 521 home runs. His dedication to perfecting his swing and understanding the art of hitting earned him the admiration of fans and fellow players.

Not only was Ted Williams an exceptional baseball player, but he also served his country during World War II and the Korean War as a fighter pilot in the United States Marine Corps. This service interrupted his baseball career, but he returned to the game each time with the same passion and determination that made him a legend.

Ted Williams' impact on the game of baseball can still be felt today. His commitment to excellence, unwavering work ethic, and love for the sport have left a lasting legacy that inspires young players to pursue their dreams. As one of the greatest hitters to ever play the game, Williams' story serves as a testament to the power of perseverance and dedication in the face of adversity.

Roberto Clemente - The Great One

Roberto Clemente, fondly known as "The Great One," was an exceptional baseball player who became a hero both on and off the field. Born on August 18, 1934, in Carolina, Puerto Rico, Clemente discovered his passion for baseball early in life and went on to make an everlasting impact on the sport. Playing his entire Major League Baseball career for the Pittsburgh Pirates, Clemente proved himself as one of the best all-around players in baseball history.

Clemente was a true force to be reckoned with on the field. He was an outstanding hitter, finishing his career with a .317 batting average and 3,000 hits, a milestone that few players have ever achieved. Additionally, Clemente's skills as a right fielder were equally impressive. His powerful throwing arm and agile fielding abilities earned him 12 Gold Glove Awards, a testament to his defensive prowess.

Roberto Clemente's greatness wasn't limited to his performance on the field. He was also known for his commitment to humanitarian work and his dedication to helping others. Throughout his life, Clemente worked tirelessly to support underprivileged communities in Puerto Rico and other Latin American countries, using his fame to bring attention to important causes.

Tragically, on December 31, 1972, Roberto Clemente's life was cut short in a plane crash while he was on a mission to deliver supplies to earthquake victims in Nicaragua. In recognition of his incredible achievements and contributions, Clemente was posthumously inducted into the Baseball Hall of Fame in 1973. Today, his legacy lives on as an inspiring example of how the power of sport can be used to make a positive difference in the world.

Nolan Ryan - The Ryan Express

Nolan Ryan, known by fans as "The Ryan Express," was an extraordinary baseball player who amazed the world with his incredible pitching talent. Born on January 31, 1947, in Refugio, Texas, Ryan discovered his love for baseball at a young age and went on to become one of the most dominant pitchers in Major League Baseball history. Playing for the New York Mets, California Angels, Houston Astros, and Texas Rangers during his 27-year career, Ryan built a reputation as an unstoppable force on the mound.

What set Nolan Ryan apart from other pitchers was his remarkable ability to throw the baseball at blazing speeds. Ryan's fastball was legendary, often reaching speeds of over 100 miles per hour, leaving batters baffled and unable to react. This incredible skill helped him achieve an astounding 5,714 strikeouts, a record that still stands today. Ryan's pitching dominance also led to seven no-hitters, another record that has yet to be broken.

In addition to his incredible pitching feats, Ryan was known for his impressive durability and longevity. He played in the major leagues until the age of 46, a testament to his incredible work ethic and dedication to the sport. Over the course of his career, Ryan was named an All-Star eight times, and in 1999, he was inducted into the Baseball Hall of Fame, forever cementing his place in baseball history.

Nolan Ryan's extraordinary career serves as an inspiration for young players who dream of becoming great pitchers. His unmatched skill, tenacity, and passion for the game have left a lasting impact on the sport of baseball. As one of the most celebrated pitchers of all time, Ryan's legacy will continue to inspire generations of players and fans alike.

Cal Ripken Jr. - The Iron Man

Cal Ripken Jr., affectionately called "The Iron Man," was a baseball legend who was admired for his incredible skill, determination, and dedication to the sport. Born on August 24, 1960, in Havre de Grace, Maryland, Ripken discovered his passion for baseball at an early age and went on to forge an extraordinary career in Major League Baseball. Playing his entire 21-year career for the Baltimore Orioles, Ripken became an inspiration to fans and players across the nation.

One of the most remarkable aspects of Cal Ripken Jr.'s career was his incredible streak of consecutive games played. From May 30, 1982, to September 20, 1998, Ripken appeared in an astounding 2,632 straight games, shattering the previous record held by Lou Gehrig. This incredible accomplishment earned him the nickname "The Iron Man" and showcased his unwavering dedication to the game of baseball.

Ripken was not only known for his impressive streak but also for his immense talent as a shortstop and third baseman. Adept both offensively and defensively, Ripken was a 19-time All-Star and two-time American League MVP. He finished his career with 3,184 hits, 431 home runs, and a .276 batting average, earning him a well-deserved place among baseball's all-time greats.

Cal Ripken Jr.'s legacy as a baseball player serves as an example of what can be achieved through hard work, commitment, and perseverance. His love for the game and incredible endurance have left a lasting impact on the sport of baseball. As one of the most admired and respected players in history, Ripken's story continues to inspire young athletes to pursue their dreams and give their all, both on and off the field.

Mickey Mantle - The Commerce Comet

Mickey Mantle, often referred to as "The Commerce Comet"

or simply "The Mick," was a sensational baseball player who became a symbol of power and grace on the baseball field. Born on October 20, 1931, in Spavinaw, Oklahoma, Mantle found his calling in baseball and went on to become one of the most beloved players in Major League Baseball history. Playing his entire 18-year career for the New York Yankees, Mantle left an indelible mark on the sport and captured the hearts of fans everywhere.

Mickey Mantle was known for his incredible talent as a switch-hitter and center fielder. His extraordinary combination of speed, power, and skill made him a force to be reckoned with at the plate and in the outfield. Over the course of his career, Mantle amassed an impressive 536 home runs, a .298 batting average, and 1,509 RBIs. His remarkable achievements on the field led him to be named an All-Star 20 times and earned him three American League MVP titles.

In addition to his individual accomplishments, Mickey Mantle was an essential part of the powerhouse Yankees teams of the 1950s and 1960s. During his tenure with the team, Mantle helped lead the Yankees to 12 World Series appearances, ultimately winning seven championships. His clutch performances in the postseason, including a record 18 World Series home runs, further solidified his status as a baseball legend.

Mickey Mantle's impact on the game of baseball can still be felt today. His incredible talent, competitive spirit, and love for the sport have inspired countless young players to chase their dreams on the baseball diamond. As one of the most iconic and revered figures in baseball history, Mantle's story serves as a testament to the power of hard work, determination, and passion for the game.

Joe DiMaggio - Joltin' Joe

Joe DiMaggio, often called "The Yankee Clipper" or simply "Joltin' Joe," was a baseball hero whose remarkable skill and charisma captivated fans across the nation. Born on November 25, 1914, in Martinez, California, DiMaggio developed a passion for baseball early in life and went on to achieve great success in Major League Baseball. Playing his entire 13-year career for the New York Yankees, DiMaggio became a symbol of excellence and an enduring icon of the sport.

One of the most famous aspects of Joe DiMaggio's career is his astonishing 56-game hitting streak, a record that still stands today. From May 15 to July 16, 1941, DiMaggio hit safely in 56 consecutive games, an accomplishment that many consider one of the most impressive feats in sports history. This extraordinary achievement showcased DiMaggio's consistency and skill as a hitter and solidified his status as a baseball legend.

Joe DiMaggio's prowess as a center fielder and hitter was undeniable. Over the course of his career, he was a 13-time All-Star, won three American League MVP awards, and achieved a .325 batting average. DiMaggio's exceptional skill and dedication to the sport helped lead the Yankees to 10 World Series appearances, with the team emerging as champions nine times.

Joe DiMaggio's legacy as a baseball player and cultural icon continues to inspire and fascinate fans of all ages. His incredible talent, unwavering determination, and love for the game have left an indelible mark on the sport of baseball. As one of the most celebrated and respected players in history, DiMaggio's story serves as a powerful reminder of the heights that can be reached through hard work, passion, and dedication to one's craft.

Ken Griffey Jr. - The Kid

Ken Griffey Jr., also known as "The Kid" or simply "Junior," was an extraordinary baseball player who dazzled fans with his talent and love for the game. Born on November 21, 1969, in Donora, Pennsylvania, Griffey Jr. grew up in a baseball-loving family and quickly developed his own passion for the sport. Throughout his 22-year Major League Baseball career, which he mainly spent with the Seattle Mariners and Cincinnati Reds, Griffey Jr. became a fan favorite and one of the most exciting players of his era.

What set Ken Griffey Jr. apart was his exceptional skill as a center fielder and power hitter. His smooth, seemingly effortless swing and outstanding defensive abilities made him a standout on the field. Griffey Jr. accumulated numerous accolades over his career, including 13 All-Star selections, 10 Gold Glove Awards, and seven Silver Slugger Awards. He retired with a remarkable 630 home runs, a .284 batting average, and 1,836 RBIs.

Griffey Jr.'s charismatic personality and electrifying style of play made him a true superstar both on and off the field. Fans adored his infectious smile, signature backward cap, and the pure joy he displayed while playing baseball. Griffey Jr. became the face of a new generation of players, helping to usher in an era of excitement and renewed interest in the sport.

Ken Griffey Jr.'s impact on the game of baseball is immeasurable. His incredible talent, genuine love for the game, and magnetic personality have inspired countless young players to pursue their dreams and enjoy every moment on the field. As one of the most memorable and beloved players in baseball history, Griffey Jr.'s story serves as a shining example of the importance of passion, hard work, and dedication in achieving greatness.

Derek Jeter - Captain Clutch

Derek Jeter, commonly referred to as "The Captain" or "Mr. November," was a phenomenal baseball player who became a role model for young fans and players alike. Born on June 26, 1974, in Pequannock, New Jersey, Jeter's love for baseball started early and propelled him to greatness in the Major League Baseball. Over his 20-year career, all spent with the New York Yankees, Jeter built a reputation as a clutch performer and a true leader both on and off the field.

As a shortstop, Derek Jeter was known for his steady and reliable presence on the field. His keen instincts, impressive range, and signature jump throw made him a defensive standout. Offensively, Jeter was a consistently strong hitter, amassing a lifetime .310 batting average, 3,465 hits, and 260 home runs. Throughout his illustrious career, Jeter was a 14-time All-Star, a five-time Gold Glove Award winner, and a five-time Silver Slugger Award recipient.

One of the most significant aspects of Derek Jeter's career was his incredible postseason success. Jeter earned the nickname "Mr. November" for his clutch performances in high-pressure situations, particularly in the World Series. Over his career, Jeter participated in seven World Series, helping the Yankees secure five championships. His ability to remain calm and focused under pressure made him a true legend in the sport.

Derek Jeter's impact on the game of baseball is immense. His leadership, sportsmanship, and love for the game have inspired a generation of young players to strive for greatness and respect the sport. As one of the most accomplished and respected players in baseball history, Jeter's story serves as a powerful reminder of the importance of determination, hard work, and perseverance in achieving success.

Clayton Kershaw - The Lefty Ace

Clayton Kershaw, often referred to as "The Claw" or simply "Kersh," is a dominating force on the pitcher's mound. Born on March 19, 1988, in Dallas, Texas, Kershaw discovered his passion for baseball at a young age and went on to become one of the most dominant pitchers in Major League Baseball. Throughout his career, mainly spent with the Los Angeles Dodgers, Kershaw has consistently displayed incredible skill, control, and determination on the field.

As a left-handed starting pitcher, Clayton Kershaw is known for his exceptional command and devastating curveball, which has been dubbed "Public Enemy No. 1" by some commentators. Kershaw's arsenal also includes a powerful fastball and a deceptive slider, making him a formidable opponent for even the best hitters in the league. Over his career, Kershaw has earned numerous accolades, including eight All-Star selections, three Cy Young Awards, and the 2014 National League MVP.

Off the field, Clayton Kershaw is recognized for his philanthropic efforts and commitment to making a difference in the lives of others. He and his wife, Ellen, founded Kershaw's Challenge, a charity that raises funds and awareness for various causes, including education, health, and quality of life improvements for children in need. Kershaw's dedication to giving back has made him a role model for fans and players alike.

Clayton Kershaw's incredible talent, work ethic, and compassion have left a lasting impact on the game of baseball. His success as a pitcher and dedication to helping others serve as an inspiration for young players to chase their dreams both on and off the field. As one of the most accomplished and respected players of his generation, Kershaw's story is a testament to the power of passion, hard work, and commitment to excellence.

Mike Trout - The Millville Meteor

Mike Trout, often called the "Millville Meteor" or simply "Trouty," is a phenomenal baseball player who has become one of the most exciting and talented athletes in Major League Baseball. Born on August 7, 1991, in Vineland, New Jersey, Trout's passion for baseball led him to greatness as an all-around superstar. Throughout his career with the Los Angeles Angels, Trout has consistently demonstrated his exceptional skills in hitting, fielding, and base running.

As an outfielder, Mike Trout is known for his incredible speed, agility, and powerful arm, making him a force to be reckoned with on defense. Offensively, Trout is a highly skilled batter with a keen eye, impressive power, and the ability to hit for both contact and power. Over his career, Trout has earned numerous accolades, including nine All-Star selections, three American League MVP awards, and eight Silver Slugger Awards. He is also a two-time All-Star Game MVP and a Rookie of the Year recipient.

Mike Trout is known for his incredible work ethic, dedication to the sport, and determination to continually improve his game. Trout's unwavering commitment to excellence has made him a role model for young baseball players, inspiring them to work hard and pursue their dreams. His sportsmanship, humility, and love for the game have also endeared him to fans and fellow players alike.

Trout's impact on the game of baseball is immense, and his achievements both on and off the field serve as an inspiration for countless young athletes. As one of the most electrifying and talented players in baseball history, Mike Trout's story is a powerful reminder of the importance of passion, hard work, and dedication in the pursuit of greatness.

Aaron Judge - All Rise

Aaron Judge, also known as "The Judge" or "All Rise," is a towering figure in Major League Baseball who has quickly become one of the game's most thrilling and powerful sluggers. Born on April 26, 1992, in Linden, California, Judge's love for baseball began at a young age and eventually led him to the big leagues. As a member of the New York Yankees, Judge has quickly made a name for himself as a formidable hitter with a bright future ahead.

Standing at an imposing 6 feet 7 inches tall and weighing 282 pounds, Aaron Judge is an intimidating presence at the plate. As an outfielder, he is known for his strong arm and impressive defensive skills, but it's his incredible power at the plate that has earned him widespread recognition. In his rookie season, Judge shattered records, setting a new MLB record for most home runs by a rookie with 52 long balls. Over his career, he has earned multiple accolades, including two All-Star selections, a Rookie of the Year award, and a Silver Slugger Award.

Off the field, Aaron Judge is known for his humble demeanor, sportsmanship, and dedication to giving back to the community. He has been involved in numerous charitable efforts, including working with children and helping raise funds for various causes.

Judge's kindness and commitment to making a difference have made him a beloved figure among fans and fellow players alike.

Aaron Judge's remarkable journey to the Major Leagues serves as an inspiration for young baseball players to chase their dreams and work hard to achieve their goals. His exceptional talent, unwavering dedication, and humble spirit have made him a role model for countless fans and aspiring athletes. As one of the most exciting and promising stars in baseball today, Judge's story is a testament to the power of determination, perseverance, and passion.

Shohei Ohtani - The Two-Way Sensation

Shohei Ohtani, nicknamed "Shotime" or "The Two-Way Sensation," is an extraordinary baseball player who has taken Major League Baseball by storm. Born on July 5, 1994, in Oshu, Japan, Ohtani's love for baseball was apparent from a young age. As a member of the Los Angeles Angels, he has made history as one of the rare two-way players, excelling both as a pitcher and a hitter.

Ohtani's talents as a pitcher are truly impressive. With a fastball that can reach over 100 miles per hour and a diverse repertoire of pitches, he's a force to be reckoned with on the mound. His abilities as a hitter are equally remarkable, displaying both power and contact skills that make him a constant threat at the plate. Ohtani's unique skills earned him the 2021 American League MVP award, making him the first player in MLB history to be named an All-Star as both a pitcher and a position player in the same season.

Off the field, Shohei Ohtani is known for his humility, work ethic, and dedication to his craft. He has quickly become a fan favorite, drawing admiration for his exceptional talents and his ability to break barriers in the sport. As a trailblazer for two-way players, Ohtani has inspired a new generation of baseball players to strive for greatness in all aspects of the game.

Shohei Ohtani's incredible story is a shining example of what can be achieved with hard work, determination, and a passion for the sport. His groundbreaking achievements in Major League Baseball have made him a role model for young athletes around the world. With his awe-inspiring talent and humble attitude, Ohtani will continue to inspire and amaze fans for years to come.

Mookie Betts - The Five-Tool Superstar

Mookie Betts, affectionately known as "Mookie" or "The Mookster," is a superstar outfielder in Major League Baseball who brings excitement and skill to the game. Born on October 7, 1992, in Nashville, Tennessee, Betts developed a love for baseball early on and has become a standout player in the league. Playing for the Los Angeles Dodgers, he has earned a reputation as a dynamic hitter, a lightning-fast baserunner, and an incredible defensive player.

Mookie Betts is a versatile athlete with a wide range of skills that make him a force to be reckoned with on the baseball field. As a hitter, he is known for his ability to hit for both power and average, making him a constant threat in the lineup. On the basepaths, Betts showcases his speed and agility, often swiping bases and making daring moves to keep opposing teams on their toes. His defensive skills in the outfield are truly remarkable, as he's able to make incredible catches and throw out runners with pinpoint accuracy.

Betts has earned numerous accolades throughout his career, including five All-Star selections, four Gold Glove Awards, and three Silver Slugger Awards. He has also been a key contributor to two World Series-winning teams, first with the Boston Red Sox in 2018 and later with the Los Angeles Dodgers in 2020.

Mookie Betts' journey to stardom serves as an inspiration to young baseball players everywhere, demonstrating the power of hard work, perseverance, and passion. His incredible abilities on the field, combined with his friendly and humble personality, have made him a beloved figure among fans and a role model for aspiring athletes. Mookie Betts continues to thrill and captivate baseball fans with his amazing talent and enthusiasm for the game.

Chapter Six:

Greatest Teams in Baseball History: Dynasties and Legends

Baseball has a rich history filled with extraordinary teams that have captured the hearts of fans and made lasting memories. These legendary squads, made up of exceptional players and remarkable teamwork, have left an indelible mark on the sport. In this chapter, we'll explore some of the greatest teams in baseball history, learn about the players that made them famous, and relive the moments that turned them into legends.

The New York Yankees (1920s-1960s)

The New York Yankees, a storied franchise in the world of baseball, saw some of their greatest successes from the 1920s through the 1960s. During this era, the team won a remarkable 20 World Series championships, creating a dynasty that remains unparalleled in baseball history. A major contributing factor to the

Yankees' dominance during these decades was the presence of legendary players who became household names and inspired generations of young fans.

One of the most famous players to wear the pinstripes was Babe Ruth, who joined the Yankees in 1920. Ruth's larger-than-life personality and incredible home run-hitting abilities quickly made him a fan favorite, and he played a significant role in the team's success throughout the 1920s. Another iconic player from this period was Lou Gehrig, whose exceptional hitting and fielding skills made him an invaluable part of the team until his career was tragically cut short by illness.

The 1950s and 1960s saw the rise of new stars who continued the Yankees' tradition of excellence. Joe DiMaggio, a smooth-swinging outfielder known for his hitting prowess, helped the team win multiple championships during his time with the club. Mickey Mantle, another legendary Yankees player, showcased remarkable power and speed, capturing the hearts of fans as he led the team to even more World Series titles. These athletes, among others, solidified the Yankees' status as a baseball powerhouse and ensured their place in the annals of the sport.

The New York Yankees' success from the 1920s to the 1960s is a testament to the extraordinary talent and determination of the players who wore the pinstripes. The accomplishments of these athletes, from setting records to winning championships, have left an indelible mark on baseball history and continue to inspire young fans today.

The St. Louis Cardinals (1940s-1960s)

The St. Louis Cardinals, one of the oldest and most successful franchises in baseball, enjoyed a golden era from the 1940s through the 1960s. During these decades, the team captured four World Series championships and was home to some of the sport's most talented and celebrated players. The Cardinals' consistent excellence in this period solidified their reputation as a top-tier team and left a lasting legacy in baseball history.

The 1940s saw the emergence of the "Gashouse Gang," a group of scrappy, hard-nosed players who brought a gritty, aggressive style of play to the field. Led by Hall of Famers such as Stan "The Man" Musial and Enos Slaughter, the Cardinals earned the admiration of fans for their never-give-up attitude and fierce competitiveness. Musial, in particular, was a true star, amassing an incredible career batting average of .331 and earning three Most Valuable Player awards during his 22 seasons with the team.

In the 1960s, the Cardinals' success continued under the leadership of other outstanding players, such as pitcher Bob Gibson and outfielder Lou Brock. Gibson, known for his intimidating presence on the mound, dominated opposing batters and led the team to two World Series championships in 1964 and 1967. Brock, a speedy and skilled base stealer, also played a crucial role in the team's triumphs, setting records and thrilling fans with his daring play.

Throughout the 1940s, 1950s, and 1960s, the St. Louis Cardinals were a force to be reckoned with in the world of baseball. The combination of their tenacious playing style, exceptional talent, and strong leadership from legendary players propelled them to the pinnacle of the sport. As a result, the Cardinals of this era have left an enduring mark on baseball history and continue to inspire future generations of fans and players alike.

The Oakland Athletics (1972-1974)

The Oakland Athletics, sometimes called the "A's," had an incredible run from 1972 to 1974, winning three consecutive World Series championships. This remarkable feat is something few teams in baseball history have ever achieved. The A's during this time were known for their excellent pitching, powerful hitting, and colorful personalities, making them an exciting team to watch and root for.

One of the most famous players on the team was Reggie Jackson, who was known for his powerful home runs and clutch hitting in important games. Nicknamed "Mr. October" for his outstanding performances in the postseason, Jackson quickly became a fan favorite. Another key player was Catfish Hunter, a talented pitcher who helped the team dominate their opponents with his incredible skills on the mound.

The A's also had a unique look, wearing bright green and gold uniforms that made them stand out from other teams. They were known for their wild hairstyles, including afros, mustaches, and long sideburns. This flair extended to their playing style, as they played with energy and enthusiasm, making them fun to watch for kids and adults alike.

Even though the Oakland Athletics' winning streak only lasted a few years, their accomplishments during the early 1970s have earned them a special place in baseball history. With their memorable players, distinctive style, and incredible success on the field, the A's of this era continue to inspire young fans and serve as a shining example of what can be achieved through hard work and teamwork.

The Cincinnati Reds (1975-1976)

The Cincinnati Reds were an unstoppable force in the world of baseball during the mid-1970s. Nicknamed the "Big Red Machine," the team had an incredible lineup of talented players who dominated the sport in 1975 and 1976, winning back-to-back World Series championships. This legendary team was known for its powerful hitting, strong pitching, and exciting style of play, making them a favorite among young baseball fans.

One of the biggest stars on the team was Pete Rose, a charismatic and hardworking player who earned the nickname "Charlie Hustle" for his nonstop effort on the field. Rose was a versatile player who could play multiple positions, and he was a fantastic hitter, setting records for career hits and games played. Another key player was Johnny Bench, considered one of the best catchers in baseball history. Bench was known for his strong arm and ability to hit home runs, making him a crucial part of the team's success.

The Reds also had a great manager in Sparky Anderson, who was known for his smart decision-making and ability to motivate his players. Anderson helped guide the team to victory by creating a winning atmosphere and pushing his players to reach their full potential. His leadership played a major role in the Reds' amazing run during the 1970s.

The Cincinnati Reds of 1975 and 1976 will always be remembered as one of the greatest teams in baseball history. Their incredible talent, exciting playing style, and unmatched success on the field made them an inspiration for young fans everywhere. The "Big Red Machine" continues to be a symbol of excellence in the world of baseball and a reminder of what can be achieved with hard work, determination, and teamwork.

The New York Yankees (1998-2000)

In the late 1990s, the New York Yankees were a powerhouse in the world of baseball, winning three consecutive World Series titles from 1998 to 2000. This remarkable team was known for its strong roster of skilled players, excellent teamwork, and ability to perform under pressure. For young baseball fans, the late 90s Yankees were an exciting team to watch and an example of what could be achieved with hard work and determination.

One of the key players on the team was shortstop Derek Jeter, who quickly became a fan favorite for his impressive hitting and smooth fielding skills. Jeter was known for his clutch performances in big games, earning the nickname "Captain Clutch." Another important player during this era was Mariano Rivera, one of the greatest closers in baseball history. Rivera's incredible pitching skills and calm demeanor on the mound helped secure many victories for the Yankees in tight situations.

The team was also known for its strong lineup of power hitters, including Bernie Williams, Tino Martinez, and Paul O'Neill. Together, these players helped the Yankees dominate their opponents with a combination of home runs and solid defense. The team's manager, Joe Torre, was an excellent leader who helped guide the Yankees to their impressive string of championships. Torre's calm and steady leadership style played a significant role in the team's success during this time.

The late 90s Yankees will always be remembered as one of the greatest teams in baseball history. Their incredible talent, teamwork, and ability to perform in high-pressure situations made them an inspiration for young fans everywhere. The legacy of this amazing team continues to live on, inspiring future generations of baseball players and fans to strive for greatness.

As you delve deeper into the world of baseball, you'll uncover even more stories of legendary teams and the remarkable players who led them to glory. These tales of triumph and perseverance will inspire and entertain young fans of America's favorite pastime.

Chapter Seven:

The Most Amazing Games
in Baseball History

Baseball has been played for over a century, and throughout that time, there have been some truly incredible games that have left fans on the edge of their seats. These games have provided moments of magic, inspiration, and sheer excitement. In this chapter, we will explore ten of the greatest games in baseball history, which have not only entertained fans but have also made a lasting impact on the sport. So, let's dive into the thrilling world of baseball and relive some of the most amazing games ever played!

1956 World Series, Game 5 - Don Larsen's Perfect Game:

The 1956 World Series featured the New York Yankees and the Brooklyn Dodgers, two powerhouse teams of the era. Game 5 of the series would go down in history as one of the most amazing games ever played, thanks to a remarkable pitching performance by Yankees' pitcher Don Larsen.

Larsen, a journeyman pitcher with an up-and-down career, was not expected to be the star of the series. However, on October 8, 1956, he took the mound at Yankee Stadium and proceeded to pitch the game of his life. He was perfect, not allowing a single baserunner, as he retired all 27 batters he faced. To this day, Larsen's perfect game remains the only one ever thrown in World Series history.

The Yankees' offense provided Larsen with enough run support, scoring two runs in the game, thanks to a Mickey Mantle home run and an RBI single by Hank Bauer. But it was Larsen's performance that captured the imagination of baseball fans. His incredible feat helped the Yankees win the series in seven games and etched his name in the annals of baseball history. Game 5 of the 1956 World Series will forever be remembered for Don Larsen's perfect game, a testament to the unexpected moments of greatness that make baseball so captivating.

1975 World Series, Game 6 - Fisk's Walk-off Home Run:

The 1975 World Series pitted the Boston Red Sox against the Cincinnati Reds in a classic battle of two great teams. Game 6 of the series, played on October 21, 1975, at Fenway Park in Boston, is widely regarded as one of the most exciting and memorable games in baseball history.

The game featured numerous lead changes and dramatic moments, including a game-tying three-run homer by Red Sox outfielder Bernie Carbo in the bottom of the eighth inning, which sent the Fenway faithful into a frenzy. The game remained tied 6-6 and went into extra innings, adding to the tension and excitement.

In the bottom of the 12th inning, Red Sox catcher Carlton Fisk stepped up to the plate. The iconic moment came when Fisk hit a deep fly ball down the left-field line. As he watched the ball soar through the air, Fisk famously waved his arms, trying to will the ball to stay fair. The ball struck the foul pole, giving the Red Sox a thrilling 7-6 walk-off victory and forcing a decisive Game 7.

Although the Reds would ultimately win the 1975 World Series, Game 6 remains a cherished memory for baseball fans, symbolizing the passion and drama that make the sport so special. The image of Fisk waving his arms, urging the ball to stay fair, is an enduring symbol of the excitement and emotion of October baseball.

1986 World Series, Game 6 - The Buckner Error:

The 1986 World Series featured the New York Mets and the Boston Red Sox, two teams hungry for a championship. Game 6, played on October 25, 1986, at Shea Stadium in New York, has become one of the most memorable games in baseball history due to an incredible comeback and a stunning error.

The Red Sox were leading the series 3-2 and appeared poised to win their first championship since 1918. Boston took a 5-3 lead into the bottom of the 10th inning, and with just one strike away from victory, the Red Sox seemed destined to break the infamous

"Curse of the Bambino." However, the Mets refused to go down without a fight.

New York staged a dramatic comeback in the bottom of the 10th inning, tying the game 5-5 with a series of hits and a wild pitch. Then, in one of the most unforgettable moments in baseball history, Mets outfielder Mookie Wilson hit a slow ground ball down the first base line. Red Sox first baseman Bill Buckner, a reliable veteran, went to field the ball, but it somehow rolled between his legs and into right field. Ray Knight, who was on second base, raced around to score the winning run, giving the Mets a stunning 6-5 victory and forcing a Game 7.

The Mets went on to win Game 7 and the World Series, while the Red Sox were left to ponder what might have been. Buckner's error became an enduring symbol of the Red Sox's championship drought, which finally ended in 2004. Game 6 of the 1986 World Series remains a testament to the unpredictable nature of baseball and the importance of never giving up, even when the odds seem insurmountable.

1991 World Series, Game 7 - Gene Larkin's Walk-off:

The 1991 World Series is often regarded as one of the best ever, featuring the Minnesota Twins and the Atlanta Braves. Both teams had finished in last place the previous year, making their appearance in the World Series a surprising and exciting matchup. The series was incredibly competitive, with five games decided by just one run. Game 7, played on October 27, 1991, at the

Metrodome in Minneapolis, was a nail-biter that has gone down in history as one of the most thrilling games ever played.

The pitching duel between Minnesota's Jack Morris and Atlanta's John Smoltz was the highlight of the game, with both pitchers putting up zeroes on the scoreboard through the first nine innings. Morris, a Minnesota native, was especially impressive, throwing a 10-inning shutout and refusing to be taken out of the game despite the high pressure and mounting pitch count.

The game remained scoreless going into the bottom of the 10th inning, with tension in the Metrodome reaching a fever pitch. The Twins managed to load the bases with just one out, and Gene Larkin stepped up to the plate. Larkin, a role player for the Twins, was not expected to be the hero of the game. But with one swing, he etched his name into baseball lore. Larkin hit a fly ball to left-center field that dropped in for a hit, allowing Dan Gladden to score the winning run and giving the Twins a thrilling 1-0 victory and their second World Series title in five years.

Game 7 of the 1991 World Series is remembered not only for its tense, scoreless innings but also for the outstanding performance of Jack Morris and the unlikely heroics of Gene Larkin. The game stands as a testament to the unpredictable nature of baseball and the power of determination and resilience.

1993 World Series, Game 6 - Joe Carter's Walk-off Home Run:

The 1993 World Series featured a thrilling matchup between

the defending champion Toronto Blue Jays and the Philadelphia Phillies. The series was full of high-scoring games and dramatic moments, but Game 6, played on October 23, 1993, at the SkyDome in Toronto, stands out as one of the most memorable games in World Series history.

The game was a back-and-forth battle, with both teams trading the lead throughout the contest. Heading into the bottom of the ninth inning, the Phillies were ahead 6-5, just three outs away from forcing a decisive Game 7. Philadelphia's closer, Mitch Williams, took the mound, hoping to shut down the potent Blue Jays lineup and keep their World Series hopes alive.

Toronto's first two batters reached base, setting the stage for Joe Carter, one of the Blue Jays' top sluggers. With a 2-2 count, Carter connected with a pitch from Williams, sending the ball deep into left field. As the ball cleared the fence, Carter jubilantly jumped and pumped his fists as he rounded the bases, knowing he had just hit a series-clinching, walk-off home run. His teammates mobbed him at home plate, celebrating their 8-6 victory and back-to-back World Series titles.

Joe Carter's walk-off home run is one of the most iconic moments in baseball history, as it is only the second time a World Series has ended on a home run (the first being Bill Mazeroski's in 1960). Game 6 of the 1993 World Series will forever be remembered for Carter's heroics and the excitement it brought to fans in Toronto and around the world.

2001 World Series, Game 7 - Luis Gonzalez's Walk-off Hit:

The 2001 World Series was a dramatic showdown between the New York Yankees, who were looking to win their fourth consecutive title, and the Arizona Diamondbacks, who were making their World Series debut in just their fourth season as a franchise. The series was filled with memorable moments and was played in the shadow of the September 11 attacks, adding a deeper emotional resonance to the games. Game 7, played on November 4, 2001, at Bank One Ballpark in Phoenix, proved to be one of the most thrilling and unforgettable games in baseball history.

The game was a pitchers' duel from the start, with New York's Roger Clemens and Arizona's Curt Schilling each delivering strong performances. The score remained tied 1-1 until the top of the eighth inning when Alfonso Soriano hit a go-ahead solo home run for the Yankees. New York's legendary closer, Mariano Rivera, entered the game in the eighth inning to try and secure the victory for the Yankees.

However, the resilient Diamondbacks refused to give in. In the bottom of the ninth inning, they mounted an improbable comeback against Rivera, widely considered the greatest closer of all time. Arizona's Mark Grace led off with a single, followed by a bunt that resulted in a throwing error, putting runners on first and second with no outs. A sacrifice bunt and an intentional walk loaded the bases, setting the stage for Luis Gonzalez.

Gonzalez, a fan-favorite in Arizona, stepped up to the plate

72

with the bases loaded and one out. He managed to fight off a tough inside cutter from Rivera, lofting a soft fly ball just over the outstretched glove of Yankees shortstop Derek Jeter. The game-winning hit dropped into shallow left-center field, allowing Jay Bell to score the winning run and giving the Diamondbacks a 3-2 victory in Game 7 and their first World Series title.

The 2001 World Series Game 7 stands as a testament to the never-give-up attitude in sports and remains an enduring moment in baseball history. The Diamondbacks' triumph over the heavily favored Yankees added another thrilling chapter to the storied legacy of Game 7 showdowns.

2005 American League Championship Series, Game 4 – A.J. Pierzynski's Heads Up Play

The 2005 American League Championship Series (ALCS) featured the Chicago White Sox and the Los Angeles Angels, two talented teams vying for a chance to play in the World Series. Though not a World Series game, Game 4 of the 2005 ALCS was a contest filled with drama, tension, and an unforgettable play that would go down in baseball history. Played on October 12, 2005, at Angel Stadium in Anaheim, this game proved to be a turning point in the series.

Both teams were evenly matched, making it a nail-biting contest. White Sox starter Freddy Garcia and Angels pitcher Ervin Santana both had strong outings, keeping the game tight until the late innings. The White Sox managed to score first, putting two runs on the board in the top of the fifth inning. The Angels responded with a run in the bottom of the fifth and added another run in the eighth, tying the game at 2-2.

As the game went into extra innings, the tension only grew. It wasn't until the top of the ninth inning when controversy struck. With two outs and no one on base, White Sox catcher A.J. Pierzynski swung at a low pitch from Angels reliever Kelvim Escobar and seemingly struck out to end the inning. However, Pierzynski quickly realized that the ball may have hit the ground before being caught by Angels catcher Josh Paul. Pierzynski sprinted to first base while the Angels left the field, believing the inning was over.

After a brief conference, the umpires ruled that the ball had indeed hit the ground, making it a live ball and allowing Pierzynski to reach first base safely. The decision stunned the Angels and their fans. White Sox pinch-runner Pablo Ozuna promptly stole second base, and then scored on a single by Joe Crede, giving the White Sox a 3-2 lead.

Closer Bobby Jenks sealed the victory for the White Sox in the bottom of the ninth, and the team went on to win the ALCS in five games. They then swept the Houston Astros in the World Series, capturing their first championship in 88 years. Game 4 of the 2005 ALCS remains a pivotal moment in White Sox history and a perfect example of how a single play can change the course of a series.

2011 World Series, Game 6 - David Freese's Heroics:

The 2011 World Series was a thrilling matchup between the Texas Rangers and the St. Louis Cardinals, with Game 6 going down as one of the most exciting and memorable games in baseball history. On October 27, 2011, fans at Busch Stadium in St. Louis witnessed a game that was filled with dramatic twists, comebacks, and unforgettable moments.

The Rangers, looking to win their first-ever World Series title, held a 3-2 series lead going into Game 6. The game was a rollercoaster ride, with both teams trading leads throughout the night. By the time the ninth inning rolled around, the Rangers were ahead 7-5, and they were just one out away from clinching the championship.

With two runners on base and the Cardinals down to their last strike, hometown hero David Freese stepped up to the plate. Freese hit a towering fly ball to right field, which appeared to be a routine out. However, Rangers outfielder Nelson Cruz misjudged the ball, allowing it to drop in and both runners to score, tying the game at 7-7. The ecstatic St. Louis crowd roared as the game went into extra innings.

In the top of the 10th inning, the Rangers regained the lead with a solo home run by Josh Hamilton. But the Cardinals refused to go down quietly, as Lance Berkman came through with a game-tying single in the bottom of the 10th, once again with two outs and two strikes. The miraculous comeback energized the Cardinals and their fans, setting the stage for a storybook finish.

In the bottom of the 11th inning, David Freese stepped up to the plate once more. With the count at 3-2, Freese crushed a walk-off home run to center field, sending the crowd into a frenzy and giving the Cardinals an unforgettable 10-9 victory. Freese's heroics forced a decisive Game 7, which the Cardinals went on to win, securing their 11th World Series championship.

Game 6 of the 2011 World Series will always be remembered for its dramatic comebacks, David Freese's clutch performance, and the never-say-die attitude of the St. Louis Cardinals. It remains a shining example of why baseball is known as America's pastime and a testament to the excitement and unpredictability of the game.

2016 World Series, Game 7 - Cubs Break the Curse:

The 2016 World Series Game 7 is considered one of the most thrilling and historic games in baseball history. On November 2, 2016, the Chicago Cubs faced off against the Cleveland Indians at Progressive Field in Cleveland, Ohio. Both teams were looking to end their long-standing championship droughts, with the Cubs seeking their first title in 108 years and the Indians aiming for their first championship in 68 years.

The game got off to an exciting start, with the Cubs taking an early 1-0 lead in the first inning thanks to a leadoff home run by Dexter Fowler. The teams traded runs throughout the game, and by the end of the eighth inning, the score was tied at 6-6. The tension and excitement in the stadium were palpable, as both teams' fans knew that they were witnessing a game for the ages.

Adding to the drama, a brief rain delay occurred before the start of the 10th inning. This pause in the action gave both teams a chance to regroup and set the stage for an unforgettable finish. When play resumed, the Cubs quickly loaded the bases and scored two crucial runs, taking an 8-6 lead into the bottom of the 10th.

The Indians, however, were not ready to concede defeat. They managed to score one run in the bottom half of the inning, narrowing the gap to 8-7. But the Cubs' closer, Mike Montgomery, stepped up and recorded the final out, sealing the victory for Chicago and ending the longest championship drought in North American professional sports history.

The Cubs' victory in Game 7 of the 2016 World Series was a momentous event not only for the team but also for their loyal fans, who had waited over a century for a championship. The game's thrilling conclusion, coupled with the historical significance of the Cubs' win, has cemented its status as one of the most amazing games in baseball history. It is a testament to the power of perseverance and the sheer unpredictability that makes baseball such a beloved sport.

2020 National League Wild Card Series, Game 3 - Padres Historic Comeback:

The 2020 National League Wild Card Series Game 3 was an unforgettable matchup between the St. Louis Cardinals and the San Diego Padres. The winner-take-all contest took place on October 2,

2020, at Petco Park in San Diego, California. Due to the unique circumstances of the 2020 season, the playoffs featured an expanded 16-team format, and this series was the first-ever Wild Card round with a best-of-three setup.

Entering Game 3, the series was tied at one game apiece, with the Cardinals winning Game 1 and the Padres taking Game 2. Both teams were eager to advance to the National League Division Series, and the anticipation was evident from the very first pitch. The game began as a pitcher's duel, with both starters, Jack Flaherty for the Cardinals and Craig Stammen for the Padres, keeping the opposing offenses in check through the early innings.

However, the Padres' potent lineup came alive in the bottom of the fourth inning, scoring four runs to take a commanding 4-0 lead. The Cardinals, though, were not about to go down without a fight. They rallied in the top of the sixth inning, scoring two runs to cut the deficit to 4-2. The game's intensity continued to build as both teams refused to give in, creating an electrifying atmosphere.

In the bottom of the seventh inning, the Padres added an insurance run to make the score 5-2. From that point on, the Padres' bullpen took control of the game. San Diego relievers Trevor Rosenthal and Drew Pomeranz, among others, combined to hold the Cardinals scoreless for the remainder of the contest.

When the final out was recorded, the Padres emerged victorious, winning the game 5-2 and securing their first playoff series win since 1998. This dramatic Wild Card matchup showcased the resiliency and determination of both teams, but ultimately, it was the Padres who moved on to the next round. Game 3 of the 2020 National League Wild Card Series will forever be remembered as an extraordinary example of playoff baseball's high-stakes excitement and a true testament to the spirit of competition.

Chapter Eight:

The Art of Hitting: Techniques and Tips to Improve Your Swing

If you're a baseball fan or player, you know that hitting is one of the most exciting and important parts of the game. Whether it's connecting with the ball for a game-winning home run or just getting a solid hit to bring in a run, it's a skill that can make a huge difference. In this chapter, we'll dive into the art of hitting, exploring the techniques and tips that can help you improve your swing and become a better hitter.

The Basic Stance and Grip

Before we start talking about swinging, it's important to understand the basic stance and grip you should use when you're up to bat.

Stance:

Stand with your feet shoulder-width apart, with your toes

pointing straight ahead.

Bend your knees slightly and lean your upper body forward a little.

Keep your weight balanced on the balls of your feet, so you're ready to move quickly.

Make sure your head is level and your eyes are focused on the pitcher.

Grip:

Hold the bat with both hands, with your fingers wrapped around the handle.

The knuckles of your top hand should be lined up with the knuckles of your bottom hand.

Make sure your grip is firm but not too tight – you want to be able to control the bat without squeezing it so hard that your hands tense up.

The Load and Stride

Now that you have the proper stance and grip, it's time to start thinking about the swing itself. The first two steps are the load and stride.

Load:

As the pitcher starts their windup, shift your weight to your back foot.

Turn your front shoulder slightly inward, toward the catcher, while keeping your head level and eyes on the pitcher.

Stride:

As the pitcher releases the ball, start your stride by stepping forward with your front foot.

Your stride should be smooth and controlled, with your foot landing gently as the ball approaches the plate.

The Swing

Once you've completed your stride, it's time to swing. There are three main phases to the swing: the launch, contact, and follow-through.

Launch:

Begin your swing by rotating your hips and transferring your weight from your back foot to your front foot.

Your hands should stay back, close to your body, as your hips rotate.

Contact:

As your hips continue to rotate, extend your arms and bring the bat through the strike zone.

Keep your eyes on the ball and try to make contact with the center of the bat.

Your front arm should be fully extended and your back arm slightly bent at contact.

Follow-through:

After making contact with the ball, continue your swing by following through with your arms and body.

Your hips should finish facing the pitcher, and your hands should end up above your front shoulder.

Timing and Adjustments

One of the most challenging aspects of hitting is timing – knowing when to start your swing so you can make solid contact with the ball. Here are some tips for working on your timing:

Watch the pitcher closely and try to pick up on their release point – the point where they let go of the ball.

Practice your swing in slow motion, focusing on each phase and making sure your movements are smooth and fluid.

Adjust your stride and swing based on the type of pitch – for example, start your stride a little earlier for a fastball or wait a bit longer for a curveball.

Practice Drills

The key to becoming a better hitter is practice, practice, practice! Here are some drills you can do to work on your swing and improve your hitting skills:

Tee work:

Set up a batting tee and practice hitting balls off the tee, focusing on proper form and making solid contact with the center of the bat.

Soft toss:

Have a partner or coach toss balls to you from the side, allowing you to work on your timing and swing mechanics without the pressure of facing a live pitcher.

Batting cage:

Visit a local batting cage and practice hitting pitches at different speeds and locations. This will help you get comfortable with various types of pitches and work on adjusting your swing accordingly.

Dry swings:

Even without a ball, you can practice your swing mechanics, focusing on your stance, grip, load, stride, and follow-through. Visualize hitting the ball and making solid contact as you go through the motions.

Mental Approach and Mindset

In addition to working on your physical skills, becoming a better hitter also involves developing a strong mental approach and mindset. Here are some tips for staying focused and confident at the plate:

Have a plan:

Before each at-bat, think about what you want to accomplish and what kind of pitch you're looking for. This will help you stay focused and ready to react when the right pitch comes your way.

Stay positive:

Baseball is a game of failure – even the best hitters only succeed about 30% of the time. Focus on learning from your mistakes and staying positive, even when things aren't going your way.

Visualize success:

Before stepping up to the plate, take a moment to visualize yourself hitting the ball hard and driving it into the field. This mental rehearsal can help boost your confidence and improve your performance.

Tips from the Pros

Finally, here are some tips from professional baseball players to help you become a better hitter:

Keep it simple:

Focus on the fundamentals and avoid trying to do too much at the plate. Sometimes, less is more when it comes to hitting.

Stay balanced:

Good hitting starts with a solid foundation, so make sure your stance and weight distribution are balanced and controlled.

Be aggressive:

When you see a pitch you like, don't hesitate – attack it with confidence and give it your best swing.

Practice with purpose:

Make every swing count, whether you're in the batting cage or taking batting practice on the field. Quality practice leads to quality results.

By following these techniques and tips, you'll be well on your way to improving your swing and becoming a more effective hitter. Remember, practice makes perfect, and with dedication and hard work, you can become the best hitter you can be. So grab your bat, step up to the plate, and start swinging for the fences!

Chapter Nine:

Pitching 101: The Basics of Throwing and Types of Pitches

Pitching is an essential part of the game of baseball. The pitcher's job is to throw the ball in such a way that it's difficult for the batter to hit it. This makes pitching both an art and a science, with various techniques and strategies used to outwit the opposing team. In this chapter, we'll explore the basics of throwing, different types of pitches, and tips to help young pitchers improve their skills on the mound.

The Fundamentals of Pitching

Before diving into the types of pitches, it's important to understand the fundamentals of pitching. Here are the key elements of a good pitching delivery:

Stance:

Start with a balanced stance on the mound, with your feet

shoulder-width apart and your throwing side foot against the rubber.

Grip:

Hold the baseball with a firm grip, placing your fingers on the seams or across the seams, depending on the type of pitch you're throwing. A proper grip helps with control and movement on the pitch.

Windup:

The windup is the initial movement of the pitching motion. Raise your non-throwing side leg, shift your weight to your back leg, and bring your hands together near your chest.

Stride:

As you begin to move forward, extend your non-throwing side leg toward home plate and separate your hands. This initiates the throwing motion and helps generate power in your pitch.

Arm action:

Keep your throwing arm relaxed and follow a natural throwing motion, leading with your elbow and then your forearm as you release the ball.

Release point:

The release point is the moment when you let go of the ball. For most pitches, the ideal release point is when your arm is fully extended and slightly above shoulder height.

Follow-through:

After releasing the ball, continue the motion of your arm across your body, allowing your momentum to carry you forward toward home plate. This helps with control and reduces stress on your arm.

Types of Pitches

Now that we understand the basics of pitching, let's explore the different types of pitches that can be thrown. Each pitch has unique characteristics, such as speed, movement, and grip, which make them effective in different situations.

Fastball:

The fastball is the most common pitch in baseball and is typically the fastest pitch a pitcher can throw. The primary goal of a fastball is to overpower the batter with speed and minimal movement. There are several variations of the fastball, including the four-seam fastball, which has a straight trajectory, and the two-seam fastball, which has more movement.

Changeup:

The changeup is a slower pitch designed to look like a fastball but with a significant reduction in speed. The key to a good changeup is to maintain the same arm action as your fastball, making it difficult for the batter to recognize the difference in speed. This pitch is effective in keeping batters off-balance and guessing.

Curveball:

The curveball is a breaking pitch that has a downward movement as it approaches the plate. To throw a curveball, grip the ball with your middle finger on one of the seams, and your index finger resting next to it. As you release the pitch, apply pressure with your middle finger and snap your wrist downward. This creates a spin that causes the ball to break downward as it reaches the batter.

Slider:

The slider is another breaking pitch that has a combination of horizontal and downward movement. To throw a slider, hold the ball with your index and middle fingers slightly off-center and your thumb underneath the ball. As you release the pitch, apply pressure with your index finger and slightly turn your wrist. This creates a spin that causes the ball to move laterally and downward as it approaches the plate.

Knuckleball:

The knuckleball is a unique pitch that relies on minimal spin and unpredictable movement. To throw a knuckleball, grip the ball with your fingertips and keep your wrist stiff as you release the pitch. The lack of spin creates unpredictable movement, making it difficult for batters to hit.

Sinker:

The sinker is a pitch that moves downward as it approaches

the plate, making it effective in inducing ground balls. To throw a sinker, grip the ball similarly to a two-seam fastball but apply more pressure with your index finger. This generates a spin that causes the ball to sink as it reaches the batter.

Cutter:

The cutter is a variation of the fastball that has a slight late break towards the pitcher's glove side. To throw a cutter, grip the ball like a four-seam fastball but slightly off-center. As you release the pitch, apply pressure with your middle finger to create a spin that causes the ball to move laterally.

Tips for Improving Your Pitching Skills

Now that we've covered the basics of throwing and types of pitches, here are some tips to help young pitchers improve their skills on the mound:

Practice makes perfect:

The more you practice, the better you'll become at pitching. Dedicate time to working on your mechanics, learning new pitches, and refining your control and accuracy.

Focus on mechanics:

Good pitching mechanics are essential for success on the mound. Work with a coach or watch videos of professional pitchers to learn proper techniques and avoid developing bad habits.

Develop a pitching routine:

Establish a consistent pre-pitch routine that helps you relax and focus on the task at hand. This can include deep breathing, visualizing the pitch, or repeating a mental cue.

Learn from your mistakes:

Every pitcher makes mistakes, but the best pitchers learn from them and make adjustments. Analyze your performance after each game and identify areas where you can improve.

Build your mental toughness:

Pitching can be mentally challenging, so it's important to develop mental toughness and resilience. Learn to handle pressure, bounce back from mistakes, and stay focused on the task at hand.

By understanding the fundamentals of pitching, learning different types of pitches, and following these tips, young pitchers can develop their skills and become more effective on the mound. With practice and dedication, you'll be well on your way to becoming a successful pitcher in the exciting world of baseball.

Chapter Ten:

Fielding Fundamentals:
Mastering the Skills of Defense

In baseball, a solid defense is just as important as a strong offense. Mastering the skills of fielding will help you and your team prevent runs and secure more wins. In this chapter, we'll cover the fundamentals of fielding, the importance of proper positioning, and tips for improving your skills on defense.

The Fundamentals of Fielding

There are several key skills that every baseball player should develop to become a strong fielder. Here, we'll discuss the most important fielding fundamentals that you should practice and perfect:

Catching:

Catching is the ability to receive the ball cleanly, whether it's thrown or hit towards you. To catch the ball properly, use both hands and keep your glove open, with your fingers pointing up. Watch the ball all the way into your glove and secure it with your throwing hand.

Throwing:

Throwing is a crucial skill for getting the ball to your teammates quickly and accurately. To throw the ball correctly, use a four-seam grip and step towards your target with your opposite foot. As you release the ball, follow through with your throwing arm and aim to hit your target chest-high.

Footwork:

Good footwork is essential for fielding, as it helps you get into the best position to make a play. Work on your agility and quickness, and always be ready to move your feet to react to the ball.

Glovework:

Glovework is the ability to handle the ball smoothly with your glove. Practice using your glove to field ground balls, catch line drives, and scoop up short hops.

Communication:

Communication is key for a successful defense. Always be aware of the game situation and communicate with your teammates about who's covering which base or who's going to catch a fly ball.

Proper Positioning

Each position on the baseball field has its own set of responsibilities and requires specific positioning to make plays effectively. Here arc some general guidelines for positioning at each position:

Infielders:

Infielders should be in an athletic stance, with their knees slightly bent and their weight on the balls of their feet. This allows for quick reactions to ground balls and throws. They should also position themselves based on the hitter's tendencies and the game situation.

Outfielders:

Outfielders should also be in an athletic stance and position themselves based on the hitter's tendencies. They should be prepared to cover a lot of ground quickly, as they are responsible for catching fly balls and preventing extra-base hits.

Catchers:

Catchers should be in a crouching position behind home plate, with their glove hand extended to give a clear target for the pitcher. They must be prepared to block pitches in the dirt, throw out baserunners attempting to steal, and communicate with the pitcher and infielders about the game situation.

Tips for Improving Your Fielding Skills

Now that we've covered the fundamentals of fielding and proper positioning, here are some tips to help you improve your skills on defense:

Practice, practice, practice:

The more you practice fielding, the better you'll become. Dedicate time to working on your catching, throwing, footwork, and glovework to become a well-rounded fielder.

Use drills to develop specific skills:

There are many drills available to help you improve your fielding skills. Work with a coach or watch videos of professional players to learn effective drills that target specific aspects of fielding.

Learn from your mistakes:

Everyone makes errors in the field, but the best fielders learn from their mistakes and make adjustments. Analyze your performance after each game and identify areas where you can improve.

Develop your mental game:

A strong mental game is just as important as physical skills when it comes to fielding. Learn to stay focused and confident, even when things aren't going well on the field. Visualize yourself making successful plays and practice positive self-talk to keep your confidence high.

Watch and learn from the pros:

Study professional baseball players and take note of their

techniques, positioning, and decision-making on the field. By observing their skills and incorporating their strategies into your own game, you can improve your overall performance.

Work on your conditioning:

A well-conditioned athlete is better equipped to make plays on the field. Focus on building your strength, speed, and agility through regular workouts and conditioning exercises. This will not only improve your fielding skills but also reduce the risk of injuries.

Specific Drills for Fielding Improvement

To further develop your fielding skills, here are some specific drills you can practice:

Ground Ball Drills:

To improve your reaction time and footwork when fielding ground balls, try the "Triangle Drill." Have a coach or teammate hit ground balls to your left, right, and straight at you, forming a triangle. Focus on getting in front of the ball, using proper footwork, and making a clean throw to a target.

Fly Ball Drills:

Practice catching fly balls using the "Bucket Drill." Have a coach or teammate hit or throw fly balls in different directions, while you stand with an empty bucket. Catch the ball and place it in the bucket, then quickly get into position for the next catch. This drill helps improve your ability to track fly balls and make quick adjustments.

Infield Drills:

To work on your throwing accuracy, try the "Around the Horn" drill. Start with a player at each infield position and have them throw the ball around the infield in a specific pattern (for example, from third base to second, to first, to shortstop, and back to third). Focus on making quick, accurate throws and receiving the ball cleanly.

Outfield Drills:

To improve your communication skills and ability to read fly balls, try the "Outfield Relay" drill. Have two outfielders stand about 20 feet apart, facing each other. A coach or teammate should hit or throw fly balls between the two outfielders, who must communicate to determine who will catch the ball and who will back up. This drill helps develop teamwork and communication among outfielders.

Importance of Teamwork in Fielding

Fielding is not just about individual skills; it's also about working together as a team. A successful defense relies on players trusting each other and knowing their roles on the field. Communicate with your teammates and support each other to create a strong, cohesive defensive unit.

Mastering the art of fielding is essential for any aspiring baseball player. By focusing on the fundamentals, practicing specific drills, and working on your mental game, you can improve your defensive skills and help your team succeed. Remember that fielding is a team effort, so always be prepared to communicate and support your teammates on the field. With dedication and practice, you'll become a valuable asset to your team's defense.

Chapter Eleven:

Base Running and Stealing:
How Speed Can Win Games

Hey there, future baseball stars! In this chapter, we're going to talk about one of the most exciting aspects of baseball: base running and stealing! You've probably heard the saying, "Speed kills," and when it comes to baseball, it couldn't be more accurate. In this game, being fast on the bases can make a big difference and help your team win games. We'll cover the ins and outs of base running, from getting a good jump to sliding into home plate, as well as the daring art of stealing bases. So, strap on your running shoes and let's get started!

The Importance of Base Running

As you probably know by now, scoring runs is the name of the game in baseball. To score a run, a player has to make their way around the bases and touch home plate. Sounds simple, right?

Well, there's a lot more to it than just running as fast as you can. Being a smart and efficient base runner can make a huge difference in tight games, and it's a skill that every player should work on.

Good base running can:

Help your team score more runs by taking extra bases and putting pressure on the defense.

Force the opposing team to make errors or bad decisions in the field.

Allow your teammates to advance on the bases, creating more scoring opportunities.

Keep your team's momentum going, helping to create a winning atmosphere.

Base Running Fundamentals

To become a great base runner, you'll need to focus on some key fundamentals. Here are a few tips to get you started:

Always know the situation:

Before every pitch, make sure you know the number of outs, the count on the batter, and where the runners are on the bases. This will help you make smart decisions and react quickly when the ball is hit.

Get a good lead:

When you're on base, it's important to get a good lead so you can get a head start when the ball is hit. To do this, take a few steps off the base, making sure to keep an eye on the pitcher so you don't get picked off.

Run through first base:

When running to first base, don't slow down or try to slide. Instead, run hard through the base, making sure to touch the front corner with your foot. This will help you reach first base as quickly as possible and could be the difference between a hit and an out.

Master the art of sliding:

Sliding is an essential skill for base runners, as it helps you avoid tags and reach the base safely. There are several types of slides, including the feet-first slide, the head-first slide, and the pop-up slide. Practice each of these slides and choose the one that works best for you.

Stealing Bases:

The Ultimate Test of Speed

Stealing bases is one of the most thrilling and daring plays in baseball. When a runner successfully steals a base, it not only puts them in scoring position but also puts pressure on the opposing team and can even change the momentum of the game. To become a successful base stealer, you'll need to be fast, smart, and fearless. Here are some tips to help you get started:

Study the pitcher:

Before attempting to steal a base, it's important to study the pitcher's habits and movements. Look for any signs or patterns that may indicate when they're about to throw the ball, such as how they set their feet or how long they hold the ball before throwing. This will help you time your jump and increase your chances of success.

Get a good jump:

When stealing a base, getting a good jump is crucial. As soon as the pitcher starts their motion, take off running towards the next base. The key is to react quickly and explode off the base with speed and power.

Practice your technique:

Just like any other skill in baseball, becoming a great base stealer requires practice. Work on your jumps, acceleration, and sliding techniques to improve your chances of success.

Advanced Base Running Strategies

As you become a more experienced base runner, you can start to incorporate advanced strategies into your game. Here are a few tactics that can help you become a more dynamic and effective base runner:

Delayed steals:

A delayed steal is when a base runner takes off for the next base a little later than usual, usually after the catcher has thrown the ball back to the pitcher. This can catch the defense off guard and increase your chances of success.

Hit-and-run plays:

In a hit-and-run play, the base runner takes off as soon as the pitcher starts their throwing motion, while the batter tries to make contact with the ball. This can create confusion for the defense and lead to more scoring opportunities for your team.

Tagging up:

When a fly ball is hit, base runners should "tag up" by standing on the base they're currently occupying and waiting for the ball to be caught. Once it's caught, they can take off and try to advance to the next base. This can be a great way to score runs, especially if the outfielder has a weak or inaccurate arm.

The Mental Side of Base Running

Base running is not just about physical skills and techniques; it also requires mental focus, awareness, and strategy. Here are some tips to help you develop the mental side of your base running game:

Stay focused:

Baseball games can be long, and it's easy to lose focus when you're on the bases. Make sure to stay engaged in the game and always be aware of the situation, so you're ready to make smart decisions and react quickly when the ball is hit.

Be aggressive, but smart:

Good base runners are always looking for opportunities to take an extra base or catch the defense off guard. However, it's important to balance this aggressiveness with smart decision-making. Know when to push the envelope and when to play it safe to avoid costly outs.

Communicate with your coaches:

Your coaches can provide valuable guidance and insight when you're on the bases. Make sure to listen to their instructions and signals, and don't be afraid to ask questions or seek advice.

Putting It All Together: Practice Makes Perfect

Like any other aspect of baseball, becoming a great base runner takes time, practice, and dedication. The more you work on your base running skills and techniques, the better you'll become at making smart decisions, reacting quickly, and helping your team score more runs. So, keep practicing, stay focused, and always look for ways to improve your base running game.

Base running and stealing are crucial skills for any aspiring baseball player. By mastering the fundamentals, learning advanced strategies, and honing your mental focus, you can become a dynamic and effective base runner that can make a big difference in games. Remember to practice regularly, communicate with your coaches, and always stay engaged in the game. With hard work and dedication, you'll be blazing around the bases and helping your team win games in no time!

Chapter Twelve:

Baseball Movies and Books: Entertainment for Fans

Baseball is not only a thrilling game to play and watch, but it has also been a source of inspiration for movies, books, and trivia that have entertained fans for decades. In this chapter, we'll explore some of the best baseball movies and books that have captured the hearts of fans, as well as share some fun baseball trivia to test your knowledge of the sport. Let's dive into the world of baseball entertainment!

Baseball Movies

Baseball movies have a special place in the hearts of fans because they bring to life the excitement, drama, and emotions that the game of baseball creates. Here are some of the most iconic and beloved baseball movies that every fan should watch:

The Sandlot (1993)

"The Sandlot" is a heartwarming and nostalgic coming-of-age film that transports viewers back to the summer of 1962. The movie follows the story of Scotty Smalls, a shy and introverted new kid in town who struggles to fit in. With no friends and little knowledge about baseball, Scotty finds himself on the outside looking in.

One day, however, he's invited to join a ragtag group of neighborhood kids who spend their days playing baseball on a dusty, makeshift field they call the Sandlot. Led by their charismatic and knowledgeable leader, Benny "The Jet" Rodriguez, the boys share a deep love for the game and a strong bond of friendship.

As the summer unfolds, Scotty becomes more confident and learns valuable life lessons from his new friends, such as teamwork, perseverance, and the importance of standing up for oneself. Along the way, the boys face various challenges and embark on hilarious and thrilling adventures. From retrieving a lost baseball signed by Babe Ruth that's been hit into the yard of a menacing, giant dog known as "The Beast," to discovering the joys of their first carnival, the boys create unforgettable memories that will last a lifetime.

"The Sandlot" is not just a movie about baseball; it's a story about friendship, growing up, and the magic of childhood. The film's timeless appeal and memorable quotes have made it a beloved classic for multiple generations. Filled with humor, heart, and memorable moments, "The Sandlot" is a must-watch film for anyone who loves baseball, adventure, and the unforgettable memories of a childhood summer.

Field of Dreams (1989)

"Field of Dreams" is a heartwarming and enchanting movie that combines baseball, family, and the power of following one's dreams. The film stars Kevin Costner as Ray Kinsella, a struggling Iowa farmer who is on the brink of financial ruin. Despite the mounting pressures in his life, Ray is a man with a deep love for baseball, a passion passed down from his late father.

One day, while walking through his cornfields, Ray hears a mysterious voice whispering, "If you build it, he will come." Although he's unsure of the meaning behind this cryptic message, Ray becomes convinced that he needs to build a baseball field on his property. With the support of his loving wife, Annie (Amy Madigan), Ray embarks on a seemingly impossible journey, turning part of his cornfield into a beautiful baseball diamond.

As Ray's vision comes to life, he discovers that his field has become a magical place where the ghosts of legendary baseball players, including Shoeless Joe Jackson (Ray Liotta), gather to relive their glory days. As more and more spirits appear on the field, Ray embarks on a journey of self-discovery, forgiveness, and redemption.

Along the way, Ray encounters other characters, such as a reclusive author named Terence Mann (James Earl Jones) and a mysterious, elderly doctor called Archibald "Moonlight" Graham (Burt Lancaster). Each of these individuals plays a crucial role in helping Ray understand the true meaning behind the voice he heard and the purpose of the magical field he built.

"Field of Dreams" is a touching and inspiring film that explores themes of family, redemption, and the importance of believing in the impossible. With its memorable quotes, breathtaking cinematography, and unforgettable story, "Field of Dreams" has captured the hearts of baseball fans and movie lovers alike, proving that sometimes, all it takes is a little faith to make dreams come true.

Rookie of the Year (1993)

"Rookie of the Year" is a family-friendly, feel-good baseball movie that combines comedy, adventure, and the underdog spirit. The film tells the story of 12-year-old Henry Rowengartner, played by Thomas Ian Nicholas, who dreams of becoming a major league baseball player despite his lack of natural talent. However, a freak accident turns Henry's life upside down and transforms him into an overnight sensation.

While playing baseball with his friends, Henry suffers a severe arm injury. Miraculously, his tendons heal in a way that gives him an extraordinary pitching arm, allowing him to throw at incredible speeds. After a chance encounter at a Chicago Cubs game, Henry catches the attention of the team's management, who quickly signs him to a contract, making him the youngest player in major league history.

As Henry becomes an overnight celebrity, he learns to navigate the challenges and pressures of professional baseball, all while trying to maintain a normal life as a preteen. With the help of his quirky and supportive friends and family, including his mom (Amy Morton), best friend Clark (Robert Gorman), and eccentric pitching coach Chet "Rocket" Steadman (Gary Busey), Henry discovers that there's more to being a successful baseball player than just having a powerful arm.

Alongside the comedic moments and thrilling baseball action, "Rookie of the Year" also explores themes of friendship, teamwork, and the importance of staying true to oneself, even in the face of overwhelming success. As Henry's journey unfolds, he learns valuable lessons about the importance of staying grounded and remembering what truly matters in life.

"Rookie of the Year" is an entertaining and heartwarming movie that appeals to kids and adults alike. The film captures the magic and excitement of baseball, and its unforgettable story of a young boy achieving his dreams against all odds continues to inspire audiences to believe in the power of perseverance and the endless possibilities that can come from believing in oneself.

A League of Their Own (1992)

"A League of Their Own" is a heartwarming, inspiring, and humorous baseball movie that tells the story of the All-American Girls Professional Baseball League (AAGPBL), which was formed during World War II when many male baseball players were called to serve in the military. Directed by Penny Marshall, the film boasts an all-star cast, including Tom Hanks, Geena Davis, Madonna, and Rosie O'Donnell, who bring this remarkable chapter of baseball history to life.

Set in 1943, the film focuses on the recruitment and formation of two teams, the Rockford Peaches and the Racine Belles, and follows their journey throughout the first season of the AAGPBL. Dottie Hinson (Geena Davis) and her younger sister, Kit Keller (Lori Petty), are talented baseball players who join the league and end up on the same team, the Rockford Peaches. As they adjust to their new roles as professional athletes, the sisters, along with their teammates, face various challenges, both on and off the field.

Jimmy Dugan (Tom Hanks), a former major league star, is hired as the team's manager. Initially reluctant and struggling with his personal demons, Dugan eventually grows to appreciate the players' talent and dedication to the game. His famous line, "There's no crying in baseball," has become an iconic phrase, showcasing the toughness and resilience of the women in the league.

"A League of Their Own" highlights the camaraderie, friendships, and rivalries that develop between the players, as well as the impact of the league on the lives of the women involved. The film also explores themes of gender equality, determination, and the power of teamwork. As the season unfolds, the characters

111

learn valuable lessons about overcoming adversity, standing up for themselves, and pursuing their dreams in the face of societal expectations.

The film is based on the real-life stories of the women who played in the AAGPBL and is a testament to their incredible achievements. "A League of Their Own" is a captivating and empowering movie that has become a classic in its own right, appealing to audiences of all ages and backgrounds. Its memorable story, engaging performances, and celebration of the trailblazing women who changed the face of baseball make it a must-watch for fans of the sport and anyone who loves a good underdog story.

The Rookie (2002)

"The Rookie" is a heartwarming, inspiring, and true-life baseball movie that chronicles the remarkable journey of Jim Morris, a high school baseball coach who pursues his dream of playing in the Major Leagues. Directed by John Lee Hancock, the film stars Dennis Quaid as Jim Morris and is a classic underdog story that showcases the power of perseverance, determination, and chasing one's dreams, no matter the obstacles.

Jim Morris (Dennis Quaid) is a former minor league baseball player who had to retire early due to an injury. Now in his mid-30s, he works as a high school science teacher and baseball coach in a small Texas town. He has a loving family, but the passion for baseball still burns within him. When his high school team challenges him to try out for the Major Leagues if they make it to the state playoffs, Morris reluctantly agrees, thinking the chances of them achieving that goal are slim.

However, the team exceeds everyone's expectations and makes it to the playoffs, so Morris must hold up his end of the bargain. To his surprise, he discovers that his pitching arm has not only healed but has become stronger, allowing him to throw faster than ever before. Encouraged by his family and students, Morris attends a Major League tryout, where his incredible fastball speed astonishes the scouts.

Despite his age, Morris is signed by the Tampa Bay Devil Rays and starts his journey through the minor leagues, facing challenges and overcoming doubts along the way. His dedication and love for the game inspire not only his family and former students but also his new teammates, who see the value of chasing their dreams.

"The Rookie" is an uplifting and emotional movie that appeals to audiences of all ages, whether they are baseball fans or not. It tells a compelling story of overcoming adversity, believing in oneself, and the importance of never giving up on one's dreams, regardless of age or circumstances. Dennis Quaid's authentic performance as Jim Morris captures the spirit and determination of a man who defied the odds to achieve his lifelong dream of playing in the Major Leagues, making "The Rookie" a must-watch film for those who love a great comeback story.

Baseball Books

Baseball has inspired countless books, from biographies of legendary players to fictional stories that capture the spirit of the game. Here are some great baseball books for young fans:

Honus & Me – Dan Gutman

"Honus and Me" is an engaging and imaginative baseball movie based on the popular children's book by Dan Gutman. Directed by John Kent Harrison, the film stars Thomas Ian Nicholas as Joe Stoshack, a young boy who discovers he has a magical power to travel back in time when he touches baseball cards. When Joe comes across a rare and valuable Honus Wagner baseball card, he finds himself transported back to the early 20th century and meets the legendary baseball player himself. This family-friendly film combines elements of adventure, history, and fantasy to create a unique and captivating baseball story that resonates with audiences of all ages.

Joe Stoshack (Thomas Ian Nicholas) is a baseball-loving 12-year-old who struggles with self-confidence both on and off the field. One day, while cleaning out his neighbor's attic, he stumbles upon a rare T206 Honus Wagner baseball card, one of the most valuable cards in existence. When he touches the card, Joe is astonished to find himself transported back to 1909, during the World Series between the Pittsburgh Pirates and the Detroit Tigers.

Once in the past, Joe meets the legendary Honus Wagner (Matthew Modine), known as "The Flying Dutchman," one of the greatest shortstops to ever play the game. As Joe spends time with

Honus, he learns valuable lessons about perseverance, sportsmanship, and the true spirit of baseball. Joe also discovers that Honus's team is in trouble, as they face the possibility of losing the World Series due to a teammate's involvement in a betting scandal. Together, Joe and Honus must work to save the integrity of the game and ensure the Pirates' victory.

Back in the present day, Joe uses the lessons he learned from his time-traveling adventure to overcome his self-doubt and become a better baseball player, as well as a more confident and compassionate person. The movie delivers a heartwarming message about the importance of believing in oneself, the value of friendship, and the power of following one's dreams.

"Honus & Me" is a delightful film that not only entertains but also educates its young audience about the history of baseball and the life of one of the sport's most iconic players. The combination of time-travel adventure, baseball action, and life lessons makes this movie a charming and timeless classic that young baseball fans will enjoy and cherish.

The Boy Who Saved Baseball - John H. Ritter

"The Boy Who Saved Baseball" is a heartwarming and inspiring baseball-themed novel written by John H. Ritter. The story is set in the small town of Dillontown, California, where baseball has always been an integral part of the community. With a rich history of the sport and a deep connection to the land, the town's people are passionate about their local team. The novel follows the journey of a group of young baseball players who are given the responsibility to save their town's baseball field and, in the process, rediscover the true spirit of the game.

The story begins when Doc Altenheimer, the elderly owner of the town's baseball field, receives a proposal from a wealthy land developer to build a massive entertainment complex on the site. Doc, reluctant to see the town's baseball legacy destroyed, challenges the developer to a high-stakes baseball game. If the local team wins, the field will be saved; if they lose, the developer will be free to carry out his plans. With the future of Dillontown's baseball heritage on the line, a group of determined kids, led by Tom Gallagher and Maria Zavala, comes together to form a team capable of winning the game and saving their beloved field.

As the team prepares for the big game, Tom and Maria search for a mysterious baseball prodigy named Cruz de la Cruz, rumored to possess extraordinary skills. Convinced that Cruz is the key to their victory, Tom and Maria enlist his help in training the team. As Cruz shares his love for the game and teaches the players valuable lessons about teamwork, self-confidence, and the importance of having fun, the team's spirit and skills grow stronger. The diverse group of kids, each with their unique strengths and weaknesses, learn to work together and support each other on and off the field.

The climactic game is filled with excitement, nail-biting moments, and surprising twists, as the young team gives it their all in a do-or-die effort to save their town's baseball field. Through their journey, the kids of Dillontown not only learn the true value of teamwork, friendship, and perseverance but also realize that the spirit of baseball is about much more than just winning or losing. It's about the community, the memories, and the shared love of the game.

"The Boy Who Saved Baseball" is a captivating and uplifting novel that captures the essence of what makes baseball such an important part of American culture. With relatable characters, exciting baseball action, and an inspiring message about the power of believing in oneself and one's community, this book is sure to resonate with young baseball fans and leave a lasting impression on readers of all ages.

Heat - Mike Lupica

"Heat" is an engaging and heartwarming baseball-themed novel by Mike Lupica, a renowned sports journalist and author of numerous best-selling books for young readers. Set in the Bronx, New York City, the story centers around 12-year-old Michael Arroyo, a Cuban immigrant and a talented baseball pitcher. Michael's dream is to lead his team to the Little League World Series, but he faces numerous obstacles both on and off the field. Tackling themes like family, friendship, cultural identity, and the love of the game, "Heat" is a compelling and inspiring story for young readers.

Michael Arroyo's life is not easy. He and his older brother,

Carlos, live in a small apartment in the Bronx without their parents. Their father, a former baseball player who taught Michael everything he knows about the game, passed away recently, and their mother is still in Cuba, waiting for permission to join her sons in America. To make ends meet, Carlos works multiple jobs while trying to keep their family situation a secret from the authorities, who could separate the brothers and place Michael in foster care if they find out.

On the baseball field, Michael is a star pitcher with an incredible fastball, and he dreams of leading his team, the South Bronx All-Stars, to the Little League World Series. However, his exceptional talent attracts unwanted attention, and rival coaches start questioning his age, demanding to see his birth certificate. With no official records available and their father gone, Michael and Carlos must find a way to prove Michael's age before he is disqualified from playing the sport he loves.

As the brothers navigate the challenges of their daily lives, they are supported by a diverse cast of friends and neighbors, including Michael's best friend, Manny, and the kindhearted Mrs. Cora, who watches over the boys. Throughout the story, Michael's love for baseball and his unwavering determination to achieve his dreams keep him going, even in the face of adversity.

Mike Lupica's "Heat" is a powerful and uplifting tale that highlights the importance of family, friendship, perseverance, and following one's passion. With a relatable protagonist, a vivid portrayal of life in the Bronx, and thrilling baseball action, the novel is sure to resonate with young readers and sports enthusiasts alike. Michael Arroyo's journey teaches us that, no matter the obstacles we face, it is possible to overcome them with courage, determination, and the support of the people who believe in us.

The Baseball Great - Tim Green

"The Baseball Great" is a captivating and suspenseful novel by Tim Green, a former NFL player turned best-selling author of sports-themed books for young readers. The story revolves around 12-year-old Josh LeBlanc, the son of a minor league baseball player who hopes to follow in his father's footsteps. As he navigates the high-pressure world of youth baseball, Josh discovers that the path to success can be filled with unexpected challenges and difficult moral choices. "The Baseball Great" is perfect for young readers, blending thrilling sports action, relatable characters, and a thought-provoking storyline.

Josh LeBlanc's life is centered around baseball. With his father's guidance and coaching, he has developed into a talented and hardworking player. When his father gets a coaching job with a prestigious travel team called the Titans, Josh is ecstatic to join the team and prove himself on the field. However, the Titans are not what they seem. Their coach, Rocky Valentine, has a hidden agenda and employs questionable methods to ensure his players' success, including pushing them to the brink of exhaustion and encouraging them to take performance-enhancing substances.

As Josh becomes more involved with the Titans, he begins to question the ethics of the team and the lengths they are willing to go for victory. He also forms friendships with his teammates, including the skilled and enigmatic Jaden Neidermeyer, who harbors a dark secret related to the team. Together, they uncover the truth behind the Titans' winning streak and must decide whether to risk their baseball careers by standing up for what they believe is right.

Off the field, Josh faces relatable issues such as coping with the pressure of sports, dealing with school bullies, and navigating the dynamics of friendships and family relationships. Through it all, he learns valuable lessons about integrity, loyalty, and the importance of staying true to oneself, even in the face of adversity.

Tim Green's "The Baseball Great" is an engaging and thought-provoking read that combines thrilling sports action with a compelling story that explores the darker side of competitive youth sports. With its relatable protagonist, authentic portrayal of the world of youth baseball, and timely themes, the novel is sure to resonate with young readers, sports enthusiasts, and anyone who has ever faced the challenge of standing up for their beliefs.

Jackie & Me - Dan Gutman

"Jackie & Me" is an inspiring and fascinating novel by Dan Gutman, perfect for young readers who are passionate about baseball and history. The book tells the story of Joe Stoshack, a 12-year-old baseball enthusiast with a unique ability: he can travel through time by touching baseball cards. When Joe is given a school assignment to write a report on an African American who has made a significant contribution to society, he decides to use his special power to travel back to 1947 and meet the legendary Jackie Robinson, the first African American player in Major League Baseball.

Upon arriving in 1947, Joe is amazed to discover that he has transformed into a young African American boy, giving him a firsthand experience of the racial prejudice and discrimination that Jackie Robinson faced during his time. This unexpected twist adds depth to the story, allowing readers to see the world through Joe's eyes and understand the challenges faced by African Americans in the 1940s.

As Joe gets to know Jackie Robinson and his family, he witnesses the courage, determination, and resilience that helped the baseball legend break the color barrier and change the course of history. Joe not only learns about the importance of standing up against injustice but also gains valuable insights into the struggles and triumphs of a groundbreaking athlete who faced adversity both on and off the field.

Throughout the story, Joe's experiences with Jackie Robinson teach him valuable life lessons about perseverance, dignity, and the power of sports to unite people from all walks of life. These lessons resonate with young readers, encouraging them to stand up for what is right and to believe in their own abilities to overcome challenges.

"Jackie & Me" is an engaging, educational, and entertaining read that masterfully blends history, sports, and adventure, capturing the imagination of young readers while imparting essential lessons on social justice and the power of sportsmanship. With its vivid and relatable characters, exciting time-travel adventure, and insightful portrayal of an important moment in American history, the novel is sure to inspire and captivate its audience, leaving a lasting impression on the hearts and minds of young readers.

Chapter Thirteen:
Baseball Trivia

Put on your thinking caps and get ready to test your knowledge of America's favorite pastime. This chapter is packed with fun and challenging questions that cover various aspects of the game, from famous players and historic moments to little-known facts that will surprise even the biggest baseball fans. Sharpen your skills and impress your friends with your baseball expertise, as you dive into this exciting world of trivia, tailored just for young fans like you. So, step up to the plate and see how many questions you can hit out of the park! The answers to the questions can be found at the end of the chapter.

Questions

1. Who was the first African American player in Major League Baseball?

2. How many bases are on a baseball field?

3. What is the term used for a player hitting the ball and running around all the bases to score a run?

4. Which MLB team has won the most World Series championships? How many?

5. What is the name of the position that the player who throws the ball to the batter plays?

6. How many players are on a Major League Baseball team's active roster?

7. Which player holds the record for the most home runs in a single season? How many did he hit?

8. Who is known as the "Sultan of Swat" or the "Great Bambino"?

9. How many innings are in a regulation baseball game?

10. What position does the player who catches the ball thrown by the pitcher play?

11. What is the name of the award given to the most valuable player in the World Series?

12. Which team won the 2016 World Series, breaking a 108-year championship drought?

13. What is the term for when a batter swings and misses three times, resulting in an out?

14. What is the name of the professional baseball league in Japan?

15. What is the name of the annual MLB game that features players from the American League and the National League?

16. How many strikes does a batter get before they are out?

17. What is the term used for a hit that allows the batter to reach second base?

18. Who holds the MLB record for the most career home runs? How many?

19. What is the distance between each base on a baseball field?

20. Who was the first MLB player to have his number retired?

21. What is the name of the protective gear that catchers wear?

22. Which baseball player was known as "Mr. October" due to his postseason heroics?

23. How many outs does each team get per inning?

24. What is the term for a hit that allows the batter to reach third base?

25. Who holds the record for the most consecutive games played in MLB history?

Answers

1. Jackie Robinson

2. Four

3. Home run

4. The New York Yankees

5. Pitcher

6. 26

7. Barry Bonds holds the record with 73 home runs in the 2001 season

8. Babe Ruth

9. Nine

10. Catcher

11. World Series MVP

12. Chicago Cubs

13. Strikeout

14. Nippon Professional Baseball (NPB)

15. All-Star Game

16. Three

17. Double

18. Barry Bonds holds the record with 762 home runs in his career

19. 90 feet

20. Lou Gehrig

21. Catcher's gear

22. Reggie Jackson

23. Three

24. Triple

25. Cal Ripken Jr.

Chapter Fourteen:

Rounding the Bases:
Bringing It All Together

As we reach the final stretch of our amazing baseball journey, let's take a step back and appreciate everything we've learned so far. From the rich history of the sport to the inspirational stories of legendary players, we've covered a lot of ground in this book. Baseball has a unique way of touching the hearts and minds of people, creating an unbreakable bond between fans, players, and the game itself. It's time to bring it all together and celebrate the true essence of baseball – a sport that teaches valuable lessons, inspires dreams, and creates lasting memories.

One of the most important aspects of baseball that we've discovered is the deep history that surrounds the game. From its humble beginnings to the present day, baseball has evolved and transformed itself into the sport we know and love today. It's important to remember and appreciate the legends who have come before us, like Babe Ruth, Jackie Robinson, and Sandy Koufax, who not only excelled at the game but helped shape its future. Their stories of triumph, struggle, and perseverance serve as powerful lessons for young players everywhere.

We've also learned about the intricacies of the game, from the rules that govern play to the various positions and responsibilities of the players on the field. Each position is unique and requires a specific set of skills, making baseball a truly collaborative sport. Whether you're a pitcher with a blazing fastball, a slugger who can hit the ball out of the park, or a fielder with a quick glove and even quicker reflexes, everyone has a role to play. Remember, baseball is a team sport, and success comes from working together and supporting your teammates.

Throughout this book, we've also explored the art of hitting, pitching, fielding, and base running, diving deep into the techniques and strategies that can help young players improve their skills. Baseball is a game that rewards hard work, dedication, and persistence, so never stop practicing and learning. Embrace the challenge of honing your craft and always strive to be the best player you can be. The journey may be long, and there may be obstacles along the way, but with determination and passion, you can achieve your baseball dreams.

In addition to the technical aspects of baseball, we've also delved into the world of baseball entertainment. Movies, books, and trivia provide a fun and engaging way to connect with the sport, both on and off the field. These stories not only entertain but also inspire and teach valuable life lessons. Whether you're watching "The Sandlot" with your friends or reading about the incredible journey of Jackie Robinson in "Jackie & Me," baseball entertainment can be a powerful way to connect with the game and expand your knowledge.

Now, let's take a moment to think about what baseball truly means to you. For some, it may be the thrill of competition, the camaraderie of being part of a team, or the simple joy of playing catch with friends and family. For others, it might be the opportunity to challenge oneself and grow, both as a player and as a person. Whatever your reasons for loving the game, never forget the incredible impact that baseball can have on your life.

As you continue your baseball journey, remember that the sport has the power to teach you important life lessons. It can help you develop qualities like teamwork, discipline, and perseverance – traits that are valuable both on and off the field. When faced with challenges, think about the stories of the legendary players who overcame adversity and succeeded against all odds. Use their experiences as motivation to push yourself harder and never give up on your dreams.

Baseball also provides an opportunity to make lasting memories and forge lifelong friendships. From the teammates you share the field with to the fans cheering you on from the stands, the connections you make through baseball are truly special. Cherish these moments and celebrate the victories, both big and small, that you achieve together as a team. Remember, it's not just about winning games but also about the relationships you build and the experiences you share along the way.

As you grow older and continue to play and watch baseball, you may find that your love for the game only deepens. From cheering on your favorite team during the World Series to participating in your local Little League games, baseball has a way of weaving itself into the fabric of your life. Embrace the excitement and passion that baseball brings, and carry those feelings with you as you navigate the ups and downs of life.

Another important aspect of baseball to consider is the power of sportsmanship and fair play. Always treat your opponents, teammates, and coaches with respect, regardless of the outcome of the game. Remember that the true spirit of baseball lies not just in winning but also in the way you play the game. Be humble in victory and gracious in defeat, and you'll find that the respect and admiration of others will follow.

Baseball is much more than just a sport; it's a rich tapestry of history, skill, and emotion that has captured the hearts of millions of fans across generations. As you continue to explore the world of baseball, remember to cherish the moments, learn from the legends, and always strive for excellence. Whether you're swinging for the fences or cheering from the stands, never forget the magic of baseball and the countless memories it can create.

Thank you for joining us on this incredible journey through the world of baseball. We hope that the knowledge, inspiration, and excitement you've gained from this book will stay with you for a lifetime. As you step onto the field or settle into the stands, remember that you're now part of a beautiful tradition, one that spans generations and unites people from all walks of life. So, keep playing, keep learning, and most importantly, keep enjoying the wonderful game of baseball!